Break Free with DB2 9.7
A Tour of Cost-Slashing New Features

About the Authors

Paul C. Zikopoulos, BA, MBA, is the Program Director for the DB2 Evangelist team at IBM. He is an award-winning writer and speaker with more than 13 years of experience with DB2. Paul has written more than 250 magazine articles and 11 books on DB2, including *Information on Demand: Introduction to DB2 9.5 New Features*; *DB2 9 Database Administration Certification Guide and Reference* (6th Edition); *DB2 9: New Features*; *Information on Demand: Introduction to DB2 9 New Features*, *DB2 for Dummies*; and more. Paul is a DB2 Certified Advanced Technical Expert (DRDA and Clusters) and a DB2 Certified Solutions Expert (BI and DBA). In his spare time, he enjoys all sorts of sporting activities, including running with his dog, Chachi; avoiding punches in his MMA training; lecturing at a university; and trying to figure out the world according to Chloë, his daughter. You can reach him at paulz_ibm@msn.com.

Belal Tassi, BSc., BESc., MASc., P.Eng., CISSP, is a worldwide DB2 Technical Evangelist. He spends most of his time helping DB2 customers, business partners, and IBMers around the world to get more out of DB2. He has more than ten years of experience working with DB2 at the IBM Toronto Lab, including work as a software developer, as an architect for the IBM InfoSphere Balanced Warehouse, and as a technical leader in the area of Data Governance. He speaks frequently at industry conferences, initiated and led the effort that created the IBM Data Server Security Blueprint, and authored the book *DB2 Viper Strikes Again: New Features in DB2 9.5* and many DB2 technical whitepapers. He enjoys spending as much time as possible with his two children, Malik and Layal, and views the concept of "free time" as just a dim memory.

George Baklarz, B.Math, M.Sc., Ph.D., has spent 25 years at IBM working on various aspects of database technology. From 1987 to 1991, he worked on SQL/DS as part of the product planning department, system test team, performance team, and application development group. In 1991, he was part of the team that helped moved the OS/2 ES database to Toronto to become part of the DB2 family of products. Since that time, he has worked on vendor enablement, competitive analysis, product marketing, product planning, and technical sales support. Today, he is the Program Director responsible for DB2 Competitive Sales Support, and he works with customers to help them understand DB2 technology directions and uses their feedback to improve the product. When not traveling the world, he lectures at the University of Guelph, teaching relational database concepts to students. You can reach him at baklarz@yahoo.com.

Chris Eaton is a Technical Evangelist and Senior Product Manager for DB2, primarily focused on planning and strategy for DB2. He has been working with DB2 on the Linux, UNIX, and Windows platforms for more than 17 years. From customer support, to development manager, to Externals Architect and now as Product Manager and Technical Evangelist for DB2, Chris has spent his career listening to customers and working to make DB2 a better product. He is an award-winning speaker at worldwide DB2 conferences and is the author of *IBM DB2 9 New Features* and *The High Availability Guide for DB2*. He also has one of the most popular blogs about DB2 on the Web at http://it.toolbox.com/blogs/db2luw.

Break Free with DB2 9.7
A Tour of Cost-Slashing New Features

Paul Zikopoulos
Belal Tassi
George Baklarz
Chris Eaton

New York Chicago San Francisco
Lisbon London Madrid Mexico City Milan
New Delhi San Juan Seoul Singapore Sydney Toronto

McGraw-Hill books are available at special quantity discounts to use as premiums and sales promotions, or for use in corporate training programs. To contact a representative, please e-mail us at bulksales@mcgraw-hill.com.

Break Free with DB2 9.7: A Tour of Cost-Slashing New Features

Copyright © 2010 by The McGraw-Hill Companies. All rights reserved. Printed in the United States of America. Except as permitted under the Copyright Act of 1976, no part of this publication may be reproduced, or distributed in any form or by any means, or stored in a database or retrieval system, without the prior written permission of publisher, with the exception that the program listings may be entered, stored, and executed in a computer system, but they may not be reproduced for publication.

All trademarks or copyrights mentioned herein are the possession of their respective owners and McGraw-Hill makes no claim of ownership by the mention of products that contain these marks.

1 2 3 4 5 6 7 8 9 0   DOC DOC   0 1 0

ISBN   978-0-07-170301-7
MHID   0-07-170301-2

 The pages within this book were printed on paper containing 100% post-consumer fiber.

Sponsoring Editor Lisa McClain	**Acquisitions Coordinator** Meghan Riley	**Composition** Glyph International
Editorial Supervisor Jody McKenzie	**Copy Editor** Lisa Theobald	**Illustration** Glyph International
Project Manager Smita Rajan, Glyph International	**Proofreader** Deborah Liehs	**Art Director, Cover** Jeff Weeks
	Production Supervisor Jean Bodeaux	

The opinions, details on features, reported performance and compression metrics, and advice in this book are from the authors' personal experiences and are not intended to represent a commitment of feature delivery or expectations of the benefits accrued from the features covered in this book. Neither the author nor IBM is liable for any of the contents in this book. The accuracy of the information in this book is based on the authors' knowledge at the time of writing.

Information has been obtained by McGraw-Hill from sources believed to be reliable. However, because of the possibility of human or mechanical error by our sources, McGraw-Hill, or others, McGraw-Hill does not guarantee the accuracy, adequacy, or completeness of any information and is not responsible for any errors or omissions or the results obtained from the use of such information.

From Paul, George, and Chris:

During the writing of this book, Belal Tassi was in a tragic car accident. We want to wish him the best and offer our heartfelt thanks for the honor of working with him, both professionally and personally. While the road to recovery can be long, he won't be alone. Get well soon, Belal; there are more pages for you to write in our next book!
(Update as we go to press: We know Belal is getting better because just a month after his accident he is talking about work and his doctors have noted he talks too much—we like to hear that, and we agree.)

CONTENTS

Foreword xiii
Acknowledgments xv
About This Book xvii

1   The Even More Space Conscious DB2 1

     DB2 Compression Goes beyond Tables 1
         Index Compression 2
         Getting to Index Compression 5
         Statistics for Index Compression 6
         Temporary Table Compression 7
         XML Compression 8
         Support for Replication on Compressed Tables 9
     Large Object Inlining 10
         The Impact of All This LOB Data 11
         Inlining Data in DB2: Historically Speaking 11
         How LOB Inlining Works 12
         The Benefits of Inlining LOB Data 13
         Usage Recommendations 15
     Say Goodbye to the High Water Mark: New Table
         Space Storage Type 15
     Sparse Multidimensional Clustering Tables 17
         The MDC Table Enhancement Train 18
         Storage Reclamation and MDC Tables
             Prior to DB2 9.7 19
         Reclaiming Storage from MDC Tables in DB2 9.7 20

2   The Even More Manageable DB2 23

     Online Table Move 23
         How It Works 24
         Things to Consider When Performing
             an Online Table Move 27
     Transportable Schemas 28
         How Transportable Schemas Work 29
         Transportable Schemas: A Simple Example 30
     Table Partitioning Enhancements 30
         DB2 9.7 Extends Table Partitioning
             with Partitioned Index Support 32
         Table Spaces for Partitioned Indexes 33
         Unique Indexes 34

DB2 9.7 Makes Rolling in and out Data Fast 34
Utility Support for Partitioned Tables 35
Schema Evolution 36
Changing Column Data Types 36
Change Column Names in Real Time 37
Relax Object Dependencies Including
 Automatic Revalidation 38
New CREATE OR REPLACE Syntax for Objects 39
Performance Monitoring Enhancements 40
New Performance Metrics with More Granularity 40
Unformatted Event Table 42
Unit of Work (UOW) Event Monitor 46
New Lock Event Monitor 47

3 The Even More Predictable DB2: DB2 Workload Manager 49

DB2 Workload Manager Basics 50
The DB2 Workload Manager: More Advanced in DB2 9.7 52
Enhanced Granular Control: Workload Enhancements 53
Enhanced Granular Control: Threshold Enhancements 53
Enhanced Granular Control: Service Class
 Enhancements 56
WLM Goes Linux 56
Priority Aging Workload Management 58
Our Tiered Priority Aging Recommendations 59
A Tiered Priority Aging Example: Buying Should
 Always Be Fast! 60
Flattening the Time to Value Curve for
 DB2 WLM Technology 61
Sample Scripts 62
New Web-based WLM Tooling 62
New WLMADM Authorization Role 64
Query Patroller and DB2 Governor Now Deprecated 64

4 The Even More Secure DB2: The DB2 Security Blanket ... 65

The IBM Data Server Security Blueprint 66
Authorization-Related Security Enhancements 68
Separation of Duties between Database
 and Security Administration 69
Principle of Least Privilege 72
SSL Enhancements for Data-in-Motion Protection 74
DB2 9.7 SSL Supports for All Clients 75
Simplified SSL Setup 75
Support for AES Encryption of User ID and Password 76

5	**The More Extensible DB2: pureXML Goes Crazy Scalable**	**77**
	pureXML and a Trifecta of DB2 Partitioning Options for Pure Scalability	78
	Other pureXML Enhancements	83
	pureXML Gets More Online	83
	pureXML Gets More Programmatic	84
	Support for Views Using XMLTABLE over XML	85
	Parallelized Bulk XML Decomposition	85
6	**The More Compatible and Easier to Learn DB2**	**87**
	Break Free with DB2	87
	Enabling, Not Porting!	88
	The DB2 Compatibility Vector	90
	DB2 9.5 Compatibility Features	92
	ROWNUM	92
	DUAL	94
	Outer Join Operator	94
	Hierarchical Queries	95
	The NUMBER Data Type	96
	The VARCHAR2 Data Type	97
	The New DB2 9.7 Compatibility Features	99
	Parameterized Timestamps	99
	The DATE Data Type	100
	Friendly Date Arithmetic	100
	Truncate Table	101
	Character Literals	102
	Collection Methods	102
	Data Dictionary-Compatible Views	103
	PL/SQL Compilation	104
	The BOOLEAN Data Type	106
	Currently Committed: Readers Don't Block Writers. Writers Don't Block Readers.	106
	PL/SQL Packages in DB2	108
	Package Libraries in DB2	109
	CLP Plus	110
	New and Improved Scalar Functions	112
	Public Synonyms	113
	Implicit Casting	115
	Created Global Temporary Tables	116
	Named and Default Parameters	118
	Autonomous Transactions	120
	SQL PL Support in Triggers, Functions, Blocks, and Procedures	120
	Record and Collection Types	121

Contents

Cursor and Result Set Handling	123
Data Type Anchoring	124
Exception Handling	125
CONSTANT Support	126

7 The Even More Available DB2 129

High Availability Disaster Recovery Enhancements	129
The DB2 High Availability Value Proposition	130
Enhanced Support for Large Objects with HADR	130
Read on Standby Support for HADR	131
Scan Sharing	134
Statement Concentrator	136
Resilience Improvements	137
Resiliency for Read Errors	138
Resiliency for Trapped Threads	138
Diagnostic and Administration Notify Log Rotation	138

FOREWORD

We have come a long way. As one of the bright-eyed engineers who had the good fortune of working on DB2 V1—we called it DB2/6000 at the time—I've seen some great releases ship. DB2 9.7 is one of the best ever.

DB2 9.7 is the most significant release we've shipped in more than a decade. We have focused our efforts on providing value for our customers. We have included some great features, but it all boils down to some pretty basic concepts: lower the cost of using the database, make it simple to use so that we can automate everything, and maintain the industrial strengths that DB2 is known for: auditability, high availability, and security.

We've added some outstanding features to DB2 9.7. Some of my favorite new features are the compression enhancements. Our clients have saved millions with the row compression capabilities first introduced in DB2 9. There's no doubt that compression is an outstanding feature, but in DB2 9.7, table compression represents just the tip of the iceberg. Two other important components of disk space usage, indexes and temporary tables, are addressed with our expanded compression in DB2 9.7. Our technology is incredible, but it's not just *what* we build but also *how* we build it. We remove the burden from the DBA whenever we can. With table compression, DB2 9.7 offers automatic dictionary creation. Index and temporary table compression are managed by the database, which decides when and what to compress; the DB2 mantra continues to be "simple, simple, simple."

Recognizing that the DB2 value proposition is unparalleled in the industry, we also looked at how to make it easy to move to DB2 and continue to leverage vested business logic and skills from other database vendors. I hear new success stories every day of clients who have switched to DB2 9.7 and personally noted to me their excited pleasure at being able to leverage their existing investments in human capital and business logic *as well* as real savings to their cost centers.

I would like to thank Paul, George, Belal, and Chris for writing this book. They are an outstanding group whose dedication to our clients and to their fellow IBMers are unmatched. Behind them is the DB2 development team. It is a privilege, not a right, to work with good people. I get to work with an outstanding group of people who are passionate about our customers' success, are dedicated to their work, and continually deliver innovative features.

Thank you, and enjoy the book.

Sal Vella
Vice President, Development,
Distributed Platforms

ACKNOWLEDGMENTS

Yet another book in a long line of projects for which I tell my wife (and promise myself) that this is the last one; it's a promise I always make, knowing I want to break it. As always, I want to thank my family for their support and understanding along the way. I hope that when Chloë turns into a teenager, and when I'm clearly no longer "cool" in her eyes, that she reads my dedications and gets how she saved my life.

Personally, this book is for two special little girls: Grace Madeleine Zikopoulos and Tia Ephraim. The Ephraims are a family I've never met, and Tia is an angel I've never seen laugh and play. Our families are in the same "club," and although it's a club I wish on no one, my wife and I pray for the Ephraims and we know Grace and Tia will make great friends: we'll see you both again in time. We love you, miss you, and think about you two *every* day of our lives.

Professionally, I'm thanking the same old cast of characters—a lot of them are in the "ye ole communal thank-you list." However, some of the folks made me, professionally, what I am today, which I hope is good if I'm thanking them! Tim Vincent, Matt Huras, Sal Vella, Paul Rivot, Alyse Passarelli, Dale McInnis, Mike Winer, Bill Minor, Leon Katsnelson, and others (geesh: I sure do require a lot of attention), thanks so much.

—Paul Zikopoulos

Personally, I would like to dedicate this book to my son, Malik, and my daughter, Layal. They are a true joy to be around and are the best thing that ever happened to me. Professionally, I would like to dedicate this book to a great group of managers at IBM: Les King, Peter Kohlmann, Jason Gartner, Boris Bialek, Anne Marie Switzer, and Paul Zikopoulos. One of the best things about working at IBM is the people you get to work with. Thanks for teaching me so much!

—Belal Tassi

Time management seems to escape me when it comes to writing books. I'm always thankful that I have an understanding family (well, at least Katrina and the dog). You know that things are taking too long to get done when the cat and dog refuse to stay up with you. Katrina had infinite patience during the creation of this book. Even though I would go into my "it's almost done...give me a minute" speech countless times, she would nod her head in that understanding manner, which really meant she still didn't believe me after all these years. But she supported my efforts and made sure I had the time to get things done. That's why, as we approach our 25th wedding anniversary, I count myself truly thankful for having married her.

—George Baklarz

To my wife, Teresa, for her constant support. Her endless compassion and tireless giving of herself inspires me to be a better person. To Riley and Sophia: your zest for life helps me to be a better dad. To the three of you, without whom my life would be empty.

—Chris Eaton

Collectively, we want to thank the following people without whom this book would not be possible: Paul Rivot, Sal Vella, Alyse Passarelli, Leon Katsnelson, Dale McInnis, Tim Vincent, Matthew Huras, Mike Winer, Kelly Schlamb, Liwen Yeow, Bill Minor, Serge Rielau, Paul Bird, Walid Rjabi, Karen Mcculloch, Scott Walkty, David Marvin, Dirk Deroos, Mary Pat O'Connor, Scott Logan, Sergio Valenti, Kevin Beck, Conor O'Mahony, Bob Sawyer, Aamer Sachadina, and Thuan Ngo.

A special thanks to Matthias Nicola and Cindy Saracco for their excellent whitepaper on the benefits of pureXML in the DB2 9.7 release; it got us up to speed in a hurry, and what's included in this book is a reflection of their efforts. We have to give kudos to our de facto (and pro-bono) agent, Susan Visser, for making yet another book a possibility, and to one of our bosses (it's also good to thank bosses), Sal Vella, for writing the foreword to our book. Finally, to the entire publishing team that worked on this book—thanks so much. We especially wanted to thank Lisa McClain (our acquisitions editor) and our terrific editor (and scheduling master it would seem) Smita Rajan.

ABOUT THIS BOOK

The DB2 9.7 *server* (herein referred to as DB2 9.7) release is a significant one, though that shouldn't come as any surprise to anyone. In fact, all the releases since DB2 8.2 have propelled DB2 as an industry leader in ease of use, storage optimization, scalability, and more. DB2 9.7 is packed with so many really cool features (and others that aren't so cool, but important to your database) that we couldn't possibly cover it all in this short book. Consequently, we decided to get together and *vote* on the authoring team's favorite features from this release's specification. It was a tough and furious road, with lobbying by authors interested in specific technologies, grueling speeches, mud-slinging that rivals any US presidential election, and more (come to think of it, most of the mud-slinging was about each other— nothing to do with the book). Perhaps it wasn't that bad, but it wasn't that easy either. The results of this *feature election* are this book and the chapters within.

We know that not everyone will agree with our choices, and we had to make some tough ones. For example, the Eclipse-based Data Studio is now the de facto tooling (you download it separately) for IBM database servers, but we don't cover that. Nevertheless, we strongly recommend that you check out Data Studio (and the unbelievable value found in their associated Optim add-ons): Data Studio is a segue into the IBM Integrated Data Management (IDM) story and it's free!

In Chapter 1, "The Even More Space Conscious DB2," we discuss the obvious and not so obvious benefits of DB2 9.7. First, three new compression algorithms have been added to support the introduction of index compression, yet another algorithm is available for temporary table compression, and another is available for the compression of pureXML data in the XDA. These enhancements are likely to deliver some serious benefits to your IT budget, and customers using these new features tell us they make the workloads these features support go even faster! The best part? They're all delivered with near-zero DBA requirements! But that's not all. Some not-so-obvious additional storage optimization features are discussed in this chapter as well. For example, there's a new space reclamation algorithm for multidimensional clustering (MDC) tables, large object optimizations, high water mark mitigation, and more.

Chapter 2, "The Even More Manageable DB2," contains our favorite ease-of-use features. DB2 has blasted off into a whole new universe when it comes to ease of use—its inflection point being DB2 8.2, when *eWeek* reviewed it and gave it a higher administration rating than SQL Server 2005! (Yes, you read that right.) In this chapter, we discuss new features such as local indexes for table partitions (which saves space, too, by the way), the ability to evolve the database schema online, move tables online, some great monitoring enhancements, and more. In addition, we cover some features that weren't delivered in the generally available version of DB2 9.7, but since we are working on them and we think they are important, we included them in the book. For example, you will soon be able to move schemas and table spaces between databases online!

DB2 9.7 delivers some great monitoring and workload control enhancements to the DB2 Workload Manager (DB2 WLM) feature, and we detail these enhancements in Chapter 3, "The Even More Predictable DB2: DB2 Workload Manager." What's more, you can now easily roll out a simple but very effective priority tiering scheme, as well as influence an application's memory prioritization, which we all agreed was really cool in the first round of votes!

You can't be in the data management game and not be concerned about data security. Hackers, crackers, spies, oh my! It seems we're always reading about something security related. The truth of the matter is that most security breaches are accidental and not of the Hollywood movie blockbuster kind. Chapter 4, "The Even More Secure DB2: The DB2 Security Blanket," details features that helps you lock down the surface area of DB2 along with implementing two key security doctrines: the *principle of least privilege* and *separation of duties*.

Chapter 5, "The More Extensible DB2: pureXML Goes Crazy Scalable," talks about XML enhancements (beyond the fact *it's now free*)—most notably the fact that all the great scalability services for relational data (MDC tables, table partitioning, and DPF) now support pureXML data. Double your resources, go twice as fast, or support twice as many users with the same response times. You choose! What's more, these enhancements really bring XML into the fold for BI analytics, since XML data can be processed with the same scalability as relational data.

Chapter 6, "The More Compatible and Easier to Learn DB2," is by far the largest chapter in this book and details what is probably one of the boldest feature sets we have ever introduced in DB2. As we're sure you've heard by now—through various analysts and customers, and of course IBMers—DB2 can run a seriously significant proportion of the typical PL/SQL found in the Oracle Database (herein referred to as simply *Oracle*) business logic. In addition, a new CLP Plus command line can interpret a good amount of SQL*Plus scripts; cumulatively, the features in this chapter flattens the cost curve associated with database migrations.

Honestly, we think that differences become the exception rather than the rule when it comes to cross-database skills, and so on, which is why we refer to this as *enablement* as opposed to *migration*. When customers evaluate DB2 and Oracle, they often think that DB2 offers so many compelling advantages, but they have invested a lot in Oracle business logic and skill sets that Oracle acts as an impediment to the cost savings that DB2 delivers. Many of our customers have found that over 95% of their application code runs on DB2 without modification! The features in this chapter are designed to remove the final barrier to DB2.

The last chapter, "The Even More Available DB2," looks at availability beyond whether a server is responding to queries; after all, as far as we are concerned, if a server is responding in minutes when it's expected to responsed in seconds, it's not available. We talk about an amazing new feature called *scan sharing*, and we talk about resilience improvements, and more. Finally, we discuss a feature that didn't make the release but is being developed and should be delivered shortly: read-on-standby for HADR environments.

All in all, we believe that we've put together a format that allows you not only to get the technical nuances of DB2 9.7's new features, but their business purpose as well. We hope this allows you to see the true value of our latest DB2 release and understand why it's so important for you to keep current. Think about storage optimization, for example, or MDC tables, or Self Tuning Memory Manager (STMM)—*every* release has delivered significant enhancements that save hard dollars in your IT budgets, make the database perform faster, and reduce the administration burden: it just makes sense to take advantage of these enhanced features. We hope you enjoy reading this book as much as we enjoyed writing it—see you in DB2 9.7!

1

The Even More Space Conscious DB2

DB2 9.7 introduces a number of new technologies, features, and tricks that propel it even farther as the industry leader for Storage Optimization that first took the marketplace by storm with the DB2 9 release. When InfoWorld's review of DB2 9 noted "Row-level compression is a revolutionary development that will leave Oracle and Microsoft green with envy," the competitive landscape took notice. Oracle rushed to bring Advanced Compression as an add-on in its Oracle 11g release, and Microsoft introduced its own compression in SQL Server 2008. While it's outside the scope of this book to delve into the competitive advantages that the DB2 server (referred to as DB2 in this chapter) compression technology still holds over competitors' recent investments, this chapter shows how several techniques have enriched this technology with even more savings. Quite simply, while the competitive marketplace was green with envy, the DB2 research and development team invested more in Storage Optimization, since storage is such a big component of overall IT expenditures.

DB2 Compression Goes beyond Tables

Costs associated with storage are ever-increasing for data servers—not only the cost of the spinning disks, but also the personal costs required to manage and maintain large server and storage farms and the power and cooling costs associated with large numbers of disks. To reduce costs, DB2 9 delivered a unique compression capability that allowed customers to reduce storage consumption for individual tables by as much as 80 percent. For most customers, table compression alone makes their DB2 databases 40 to 50 percent smaller than they were without compression. This improves not only runtime performance but backup and restore performance as well, and it may even significantly reduce power and cooling costs.

To add even greater savings, DB2 9.7 adds more compression capabilities including index compression, temporary table compression, and XML compression—all discussed in this section.

Index Compression

In many databases, the storage consumed by indexes can be as much or more than the storage consumed by table data itself. The percentage of storage used for indexes increases even more when table compression is used, since the tables take up only 20 percent (or more) of their original size, yet the indexes still consume their full size. However, it's not as simple as just applying the same compression technique used for row data to your indexes, because index access is extremely performance sensitive. Indexes help you find row data more efficiently. If you were to introduce more overhead into this access path, you could run the risk of degrading performance.

New compression algorithms have been implemented in DB2 9.7 to compress index sizes and help improve performance. Performance can be improved by reducing the I/O during index access in a number of ways. First, it is possible simply to read in fewer pages because each page contains more index entries, and therefore an index range scan may result in fewer pages being read. Second, if the index is smaller, the index tree may contain fewer levels and therefore traversing the index requires fewer nonleaf page accesses. Finally, if each page contains more index keys, the buffer pool will contain more index keys (since the pages remain compressed in memory) and therefore the index page you need to access may remain in memory due to the increased index page buffer pool hit ratio.

RID List Compression

The first new index compression algorithm is known as *RID (row ID) list compression*. An index entry comprises a key value (the data value from the row and column making up the index) and the list of row IDs on which this key can be found. A RID comprises a page number and a slot number that points to the page within the table and the offset within that page on which the row can be found. For example, a table with three columns (COL1, COL2, and COL3) may have an index on COL1. If two rows both have a value of SMITH in COL1, the index key entry will be made up of the key SMITH and a list of the two RIDs that point to the page and slot of these two rows within the table.

RID list compression is a way to store the row ID portion of the index entries in a much more compact and efficient manner without a performance loss during data access. Since the RID list is sorted in sequence (that is, entries are kept in a list ordered by ascending RID value), a more efficient way to store the RIDs is to store the first key value and then store the delta between the first key value and the next key value. For example, consider a RID list made up of the following 6-byte RIDs:

```
<00 00 05 13, 00 02>
<00 00 05 13, 00 04>
<00 00 06 15, 00 06>
<00 00 06 15, 00 07>
```

Rather than store these 24 bytes, DB2 9.7 can store the RIDs more efficiently and consume only 12 bytes of storage for these entries:

```
<00 00 05 13, 00 02>
<02>
<01 02, 00 02>
<01>
```

Look at the first RID after compression is applied—it's the same. The second entry is the aggregate difference between the first entry and the second original entry. The only difference between these two entries before compression is the last slot number: the first entry ends in <02> and the second entry ends in <04>. DB2 RID list compression would optimize the storage of these entries by storing the difference between the page number and slot directory for each entry; in this case, it stores <02> since <02>+<02>=<04>. Similarly, the third RID value stored is the difference between the second and third keys. This compacts the space from 6 bytes to as small as 1 byte in some cases without a negative performance impact, because it takes only one additional instruction to determine the next RID.

RID list compression is most useful for non-unique indexes that would have long RID lists following the index key values. However, the best part of the new index compression capability in DB2 9.7 is that you don't have to specify when to use it—and you don't have to specify which compression algorithm to use.

In fact, if you're licensed to use table compression, DB2 will automatically compress indexes on any compressed table and automatically determine whether RID list compression would be useful. The other index compression algorithm, prefix compression, is chosen automatically by DB2 as well. Save on storage without DBA intervention? Nice!

Prefix Compression

The second index compression algorithm is known as *prefix compression*. As mentioned, an index is made up of a key value followed by an RID list. You've already read about compression of the RID list; this algorithm deals with the compression of the key value. Index keys are stored on the leaf pages of an index in sequential order (ascending if the index is created in default ascending order, or descending if the index is created the other way). This means that key values that are adjacent to each other on an index page have similar text strings. For example, an index on two columns, LAST_NAME and FIRST_NAME, may look something like this:

```
EATON,     CHRIS
EATON,     TERESA
ZIKOPOULOS,    PAUL
ZIKOPOULOS,    PRISCILLA
```

In this example, a number of key values share a common prefix, and DB2 therefore has the opportunity to store the common prefix once on the page and then refer to that common prefix throughout the index page, simply by pointing first to the prefix and then concatenating the rest of the key value. For example, the preceding could be compressed written like:

```
EATON, (1),   ZIKOPOULOS, P (2)
------------------------------------------------
(1)   CHRIS
(1)   TERESA
(2)   AUL
(2)   RISCILLA
```

By storing the common prefixes in the header of the index page, DB2 can refer to them as many times as necessary within the same page without incurring significant performance overhead—it's simply a pointer reference within the same page.

The best candidates for prefix compression are indexes that contain multiple columns and have character strings, because more repeating patterns within text columns tend to appear and typically multicolumn indexes repeat the same first and second columns several times on the same index page. Note that DB2 doesn't require that the prefix be an entire column or set of columns. As shown in the preceding example, the entire first column and a substring of the second column are candidates for prefix compression, as would be a simple substring of just the first column. This greatly expands the compression opportunities for the index. Once again, a DBA doesn't have to specify which compression algorithm to use or the size of the prefix (as with other vendor's technologies). DB2 will examine the contents of the index page and use the compression algorithm that makes the most sense on its own: no DBA hands-on management required!

Finally, although not considered a compression algorithm, DB2 9.7 adds some storage efficiency to the slot directory with a new variable slot directory mechanism on the index page. In short, instead of allocating space in the slot directory for all the possible slots in a page (whether they are used or not), DB2 9.7 only allocates space in the slot directory for the slots that are being used.

Getting to Index Compression

As mentioned, the default behavior is that any index created on a table that is already compressed will automatically have its indexes compressed. It is, however, possible for you to create indexes on compressed tables whereby the index would not be compressed, and, similarly, you can create a compressed index on a noncompressed table.

Manual index compression is controlled with the CREATE INDEX command's COMPRESS attribute. For example, to create a compressed index on table T1, you could enter the following command:

CREATE INDEX inx1 ON t1(col1, col2) COMPRESS YES

If an index already exists and you want to compress it, you can use the ALTER INDEX command followed by an offline reorganization of the index; just use the same option for index creation:

ALTER INDEX IX1 COMPRESS YES;
REORGANIZE INDEX IX1;

You can create or alter an index to compress it as long as the index is not an index on the system catalogs or a multidimensional clustering (MDC) block index which points to pages, not rows, and are therefore already storage efficient. We don't recommend that you turn on index compression for unique indexes created on a single numeric column. Why not? If an index is unique, RID list compression will not apply, and if the column type is numeric (for example, an INTEGER data type), prefix compression is unlikely to be very applicable for unique integer values. Note that you can also uncompress an index in a manner similar to that already described earlier. Simply alter the index using the COMPRESS NO option and then reorganize the index to decompress it.

We discuss temporary table compression later in this chapter, but it's worth noting here that indexes created on compressed temporary tables are always compressed (without any option for the user to create them uncompressed).

Statistics for Index Compression

As with table compression, there are statistics and administrative views to estimate the expected compression you will achieve by turning on index compression and see the actual storage savings after indexes are compressed.

A new column called COMPRESSION has been added to the SYSCAT.INDEXES catalog table in DB2 9.7. This column stores a single character that is either Y if compression has been enabled for an index or N if it hasn't. Another new column, called PCTPAGESSAVED, has been added to the SYSSTAT.INDEXES table. This column represents the percentage of index pages that have been saved by using compression for a particular index. (This column is also available in the SYSCAT.INDEXES catalog table.)

The new ADMIN_GET_INDEX_COMPRESS_INFO table function can be used to estimate the compression savings you may achieve using index compression. This table function not only tells you whether an index has had compression turned on, but also whether the index is actually compressed (and if so, how many pages have been saved). If the index is not compressed, you can use this table function to get a good estimate of how many index pages would be saved if the index were to be compressed. For example, the following query results show that the IX1 index is compressed and has achieved a storage savings of 50 percent. It also tells you that the IX2 index isn't compressed; however, if you were to compress it, you would save about 47 percent of your index pages:

```
SELECT indname, compress_attr, index_compressed, pct_pages_saved
  FROM TABLE(
      sysproc.admin_get_index_compress_info('', 'EATON', 'T1', ,))

INDNAME    COMPRESS_ATTR  INDEX_COMPRESSED  PCT_PAGES_SAVED
---------- -------------- ----------------- ----------------
IX1        Y              Y                 50
IX2        N              N                 47
```

Temporary Table Compression

DB2 9.7 also reduces storage consumption through the new temporary (temp) table compression capability. Temporary tables are created either by DB2 itself for internal processing or by users through the creation of declared or user-created temporary tables. For example, DB2 will create temporary tables to sort large result sets as part of a query that is performing an aggregation or a query that contains an ORDER BY clause. DB2 will also store a partial query request in a temporary table as part of query processing.

For large data warehouses that perform hefty sorts or aggregates over a large number of rows, temporary tables can consume a large amount of disk space. DB2 will try to perform sorts and place temporary data in memory, but if the temporary working space needed is too great, DB2 will store the temporary results in tables inside the system temporary table space. To reduce these storage requirements, DB2 9.7 can compress the temporary tables using a compression algorithm that's similar to the one used for table compression. Temporary table compression is automatic, just like table compression. (You should be noticing a trend with the DB2 9.7 features: great compression and performance with next to minimal or no DBA effort.)

Specifically, if DB2 9.7 detects the license key for the Storage Optimization feature, then any temporary table that spills to disk and is eligible for compression will automatically be compressed *without* any DBA or end user action required. Eligible temporary tables are those tables used for sorts, explicit temporary tables created in an access plan (as shown in an EXPLAIN plan as a TEMP operator), table queues used in a partitioned database environment, or any user-created temporary table—either declared global temporary tables (DGTTs) or created global temporary tables (CGTTs). In all of these cases, as long as the temporary table crosses a specific threshold and the row length is sufficiently long, DB2 will automatically create a compression dictionary (similar to table compression) and compress rows as they are written to disk in this temporary table. Of course, it stands to reason that the temp table's row length needs to be sufficiently long so that compression would be effective. For example, DB2 can sort RIDs prior to list prefetch occurring, but RIDs are too short to be effectively compressed using base table compression algorithms, and therefore DB2 would not automatically compress temporary tables that contain only RIDs.

To monitor temporary table compression in DB2, you can use the db2pd command's temptable option. This option generates a list of any temporary tables that have been compressed, as well as how many pages were saved in the temporary table space. (Note that this is a historical view and will not show you in-flight temp table compression.)

XML Compression

As of DB2 9.7, DB2 can compress XML data stored in the XML data area (XDA) using the same compression techniques it uses for base tables. The DB2 pureXML capability (free in all editions of DB2 9.7 as of February 2009) stores XML data in a preparsed hierarchical structure inside the database. This delivers significant usability and performance advantages over competitors' offerings. This XML column data is not stored on the same data page as the rest of the row, but is stored in an XML-specific storage object known as the XDA. (DB2 9.7 introduced the concept of XML *inlining*, which would allow you to store the XML data with the row and not in the XDA, but this is applicable only to smaller XML documents that can fit on a data page.) As of DB2 9.7, when a table is enabled for compression, any XML data that resides within the XDA area will be compressed. (Of course, if the XML data is inlined using the technology first introduced in DB2 9.5, it was already eligible for compression since it's part of a table's data page.)

XML compression is similar to table compression in that DB2 will scan all the XML data for that table and build a compression dictionary of the most common repeating patterns within that data (looking in this case at only the XML data in the XDA). This compression dictionary is stored inside the XDA object, and repeating strings found in the XML data are replaced with 12-bit symbols pointing to the corresponding dictionary entries. If you had large XML documents stored in a compressed table, you would actually end up with two separate compression dictionaries: one for the XDA-stored XML data and one for the table. (Inlined XML data would be compressed using the table compression dictionary.)

As of DB2 9.7, whenever a table has its compression attribute set to YES, a reorganization or LOAD operation on the table will explicitly create both a table compression dictionary and the XML compression dictionary—assuming the XML data is stored in the XDA. Of course, the compression dictionary could implicitly be created through the automatic dictionary creation (ADC) mechanism, such that if any method you use to get data into the database breaches the ADC threshold, it would be compressed. As you would expect from what you've read thus far in this chapter, this is all automatic!

From a technical perspective, you should be aware that DB2 9.7 has a new storage format for the XDA objects, and only tables created in DB2 9.7 will have this new storage format, which is necessary for XML compression. If a table was created prior to DB2 9.7 and you want compress large XML documents stored in the XDA, you must re-create the table or use the online table move capabilities (new in DB2 9.7 and covered in Chapter 2) to re-create the table with the new XDA storage format.

As with table compression, XML compression can be monitored and estimated using the ADMINTABCOMPRESSINFO administrative view. DB2 9.7 adds a new column to this view, called OBJECT_TYPE, which contains a value of DATA for table data or XML for compression of the XML XDA data within that table. The PAGES_SAVED_PERCENT column will show you either the percentage of pages actually saved or DB2's estimate of the percentage of pages that would be saved if you compressed the XML data within the table. You will see two rows for each table—one for the estimate of savings for the table data and one with an estimate for the XML data.

Support for Replication on Compressed Tables

Some users love DB2 compression but couldn't use it because they were using replication, and this feature wasn't compatible with compression. In other words, before DB2 9.7, the use of DATA CAPTURE CHANGES on a table was not compatible with the use of the COMPRESS YES keyword for that table. This was because the capture component of replication read the log records and replicated the contents of those log records to remote servers. However, since table compression results in log records also contain compressed data, it was not possible for both to work together.

The good news is as of DB2 9.7, DB2's log read interface has been enhanced so that it can now handle compressed records. Specifically, DB2 can now read a compressed log record and resolve the compression symbols using the compression dictionary to uncompress the row prior to passing the log record over to the replication CAPTURE program. Sounds simple, right? Well, there's more to it than first glance. Support for replication on compressed tables had to be developed in a way that DB2 could handle a case in which log records read from a log file that used an earlier compression dictionary could still be resolved. For example, imagine a scenario in which the capture program was reading the log to replicate data, but since that log was written, the table was reorganized and this re-created the compression dictionary and a specific symbol was no longer used because better compression opportunities used different symbols. DB2 9.7 can handle these kinds of scenarios, and, therefore, you can now use table compression and replication on the same source tables.

Large Object Inlining

Over the last couple of DB2 releases, there's been a lot of focus on large objects (LOBs). For example, DB2 9.5 introduced the concept of LOB blocking, which can reduce the amount of network flows for an application in which just 10 rows with LOB columns are retrieved by up to 97 percent!

Why so much focus on LOBs? Traditional use of LOB columns in a database involved storing a large quantity of data that was infrequently accessed within the LOB column—for example, storing an employee's photograph. Today, however, the use of LOBs has expanded from storing the traditionally obvious (video, audio, and image data) to storing loosely typed data—quite simply, a "dump bucket" for a bunch of data bits.

The movement toward LOBs for this kind of data has materialized because often this data doesn't consume a lot of space, but developers want to accommodate for those cases in which an entry could have a large amount of LOB data. Consider a comment field, for example. Of course, developers could always store comments in a VARCHAR, but then that maximum amount of data is limited (we personally hate those 1000-character limited feedback fields). The bottom line is that a LOB can accommodate free-form data without concern for what's inside the column, and that makes LOBs very appealing to developers.

A popular enterprise resource planning (ERP) application defines a lot of LOBs within its application schema, for example, as does DB2 in its own catalog tables. We're investing in LOB functionality and performance because real-world applications use LOBs to store data. Many applications define these LOBs for the largest use case, but most of the time they just store small amounts of data. These applications don't use a VARCHAR for the aforementioned reasons, but they have to contend with a bunch of extra allocation to handle the LOB when perhaps it's needed for only a couple of rows in a million-row table. This is where DB2 9.7 optimizes the performance and storage footprint of your applications that have a heavy reliance on LOB data.

DB2 9.7 extends its inherent data inlining feature to LOB data, which provides not only an even more optimized storage structure, but also extended benefits such as compression for inlined LOBs and implicit performance improvements.

Quite simply, as of DB2 9.7, you can store small LOBs within the formatted row data in a regular table (or a temporary table for that matter: both declared and the new DB2 9.7-created temporary tables are supported) as opposed to externally via the LOB allocation object and the corresponding LOB itself.

The Impact of All This LOB Data

The result of the proliferation of LOB data is that this data is looking more and more like regular data (if such a data type exists anymore), and therefore the performance expectations placed upon LOB data is also converging with regular data.

Even in consideration of the LOB blocking enhancements introduced in DB2 9.5, LOBs have an infrastructure that can "get in the way" of the fast performance expected from small amounts of stored data. First, non-inlined LOBs are stored in an area external to the data page (similar to the XDA concept outlined earlier in this chapter). Because of this architecture, when the database manager wants to access a LOB, the LOB first accesses the LOB descriptor that's stored on the actual data page (one unit of I/O), and this points to the LOB's actual location. So the database manager has to perform a second unit of I/O to retrieve the LOB. Two units of I/O to get a LOB—that can get in the way of performance for a small amount of data! Second, LOBs stored external to the data page can't be serviced by buffer pool services (prefetch, cache hits, and so on). So not only do LOB retrievals take multiple I/Os, they have to be fetched from the disk each and every time they are requested (this is not the case for non-inlined XML data stored that's stored outside the data page in the XDA).

All this adds up to a heavy infrastructure and the impediment mismatch between the performance expectations of small LOB data and the architecture that supports its retrieval.

Inlining Data in DB2: Historically Speaking

Inlining is not new to DB2. In fact, DB2 has been inlining data for a while. For example, abstract data types (ADTs) could be inlined when they were first introduced. The DB2 9.5 release extended inlining to XML data. You explicitly request inlining for ADTs and XML using the INLINE LENGTH data definition language (DDL) extension. DB2 9.7 extends the inlining capability to LOB data. Unlike ADT and XML inlining, which is explicit, LOB inlining has implicit and explicit inlining components (more on that in a bit).

How LOB Inlining Works

LOB inlining is applied to data on a row-by-row basis within a table. Consider the example INFO table created with the following DDL:

```
CREATE TABLE INFO (ID INT, PRODUCT VARCHAR(10),
STREAM_DATA BLOB(10MB) INLINE LENGTH 1000)
```

Figure 1-1 shows a great simplification on how LOB inlining works.

As you can see in the figure, LOB data associated with ID=3 is less than 1000 bytes, and therefore it's stored within the base table (and of course eligible for buffer pool caching and compression, but that's beyond the point we're illustrating here). The LOB data associated with ID=9 is larger than what can be accommodated inline and therefore is stored externally to the data page.

When you define a table with the INLINE LEGNTH option, you're *explicitly* inlining the LOB data (explicit LOB inlining is the same concept as ADT and XML inlining). You can also use the ALTER TABLE statement to add explicit inlining capabilities to an existing table, or increase the size of the inlined length. (If you want to lower the inline length, use the new DB2 9.7 online table move feature or re-create the table.) If you enable an existing populated table for inlining, or increase the inline length, you need to perform a REORG...WITH LONGLOBDATA operation to move eligible LOB data into the base table.

Since inlined LOB data is part of a base table, utilities that you run on your tables keep inline metadata. For example, if you issue a CREATE TABLE LIKE... statement, the new table will have the same inline characteristics: DB2LOOK exposes the defined inline length when generating DDL, and so on. When you run the RUNSTATS utility operation on a table with inlined LOB columns, statistics are collected and used to optimize queries on the table. Quite simply, as you would with any other changes you make to a table, keep your statistics up to date if you decide to inline LOBs on existing tables.

Base Table: INFO

ID	PRODUCT	STREAM_DATA
3	APPETIZER	»»»» »»»»
9	DRINK	←
27	MEAL	»»»» »»»»

LOB Storage Object: INFO

STREAM_DATA
»»»»»»»»»»»»»»»»»»»»»»»»»»»»

Figure 1.1 *A DB2 table with some LOB data inlined and some data stored outside the data page*

Finally, when you define a table with a LOB column using the `INLINE LENGTH` clause, if you don't explicitly specify an inline length, its value will default to the maximum size of the defined LOB that is supported by the page size in consideration of the inline overhead and other data columns in the table.

Something Unique to LOBs: Implicit Inlining

Beyond being able to inline LOB data explicitly, DB2 9.7 also introduces *implicit* inlining (which appears explicitly: say what?). Let us explain—and, by the way, this is valuable information, especially if your schema is characterized by a lot of small LOBs that are in the hundreds of bytes range. In fact, implicit inlining really opens up the usefulness of LOBs without any of the drawbacks affecting the infrastructure for small LOBs. The reason we say that implicit inlining (it's not available for XML or ADT data) appears explicitly is because it's automatic. You don't do anything to enable this—this automatic stuff is a nice trend, isn't it?

In fact, the DB2 catalog tables make a lot of use of LOBs (for the reasons outlined so far in this section), and since this feature works so well, DB2 catalog tables with LOB columns (for example, SYSVIEWS, SYSPLAN, SYSROUTINES, and more) all leverage this capability as of DB2 9.7. In fact, if you migrate your database to DB2 9.7, inlining is added to these table definitions (you have to `REORG` the table to inline existing data).

For example, let's assume you have a table defined with a LOB column that can store up to 1GB of LOB data to provide maximum flexibility to the application. A 1GB LOB column requires a 256-byte descriptor in DB2 (more on this in the next section). Implicit inlining is essentially DB2 smarts that say, "If a LOB is smaller than the descriptor, then DB2 is going to inline the LOB *even if you didn't* create or alter the table to inline LOBs in the first place." This is the kind of stuff we love: when the database just makes the right decision for us and automatically makes our infrastructure better and more nimble.

The Benefits of Inlining LOB Data

Inlining data offers multiple benefits, especially with LOB data. The first benefit stems from the fact that since inlined LOB data can be stored alongside the accompanying row data on the same data page: you can avoid the fixed infrastructure cost to storing LOBs in DB2. (Note that it isn't necessarily the case that this infrastructure is bad for all LOBS, it's the emergence of the small "dump bucket" LOB use case that's storing bytes or kilobytes of information that's creating the inefficiency.) For example, when you define a LOB column in a table, you define the maximum size for your LOB data. Based on that size, a LOB descriptor is placed in the LOB field on the data page, which serves as metadata pointer to the externally stored LOB. The bigger the maximum size of the LOB, the bigger the descriptor (from 68 to more than 300 bytes).

Let's assume you want to store a 1-byte LOB (we're using an extreme example here to illustrate a point). For DB2 to store this 1-byte LOB without inlining, it needs to store a descriptor in the data page. This descriptor is 68 bytes (the minimum descriptor length for any LOB less than 1KB). Now the LOB has to be stored; however, DB2 stores LOBs using buddy segment technology, which stores a LOB in 1KB increments (1024 bytes), making the total storage required to store this 1-byte LOB 1092 bytes. So, without LOB inlining, if all you wanted to do was store a 1-byte LOB, you'd need 1092 bytes of storage. In contrast, if the LOB was inlined using the new DB2 9.7 functionality, DB2 would need only 5 bytes (4 bytes for the inlined overhead—more on that in a bit—and 1 byte for the LOB itself).

Another benefit to inlining LOBs is that they can leverage buffer pool services to avoid I/O since the data can be cached in the buffer pool. This implicitly suggests another benefit for inlined LOB data: even if it isn't in the buffer pool, the database manager needs to perform only a single I/O to get it, since DB2 doesn't have to access the LOB descriptor and then locate and retrieve the LOB with a separate I/O cycle. For example, assume you want to store an 8KB LOB (that's about 1200 words in a comment field, or about 5500 characters). If the data was inlined, the application could get high cache-hit ratios on this data and deliver impressive performance. As a rule of thumb, from a performance perspective, expect your inlined LOBs to perform like VARCHAR column data since that's pretty much what they become when they are inlined.

Finally, since the LOB data is stored on the data page, it is eligible for compression, which is the focus of this chapter.

If you mix all the benefits together, you'll find the DB2 9.7 LOB inlining capability can deliver some significant benefits to your application. Table 1-1 details some tests with small LOBs run in our labs.

As you can see in the table, the second column shows the benefits that DB2 compression delivers. Notice that the LOB storage hasn't changed, but the base table compressed at around 35 percent (most of the data in this table is LOB data so it's not eligible for compression). In DB2 9.7, notice that even without any compression, the ability to inline a LOB has reduced the size of

	DB2 9.5	DB2 9.5 (No inlining; just compression)	DB2 9.7 (Only LOB inlining; no compression)	DB2 9.7 (LOB inlining with compression)
Base table (KBs)	24,320	5248	22,144	4736
LOB storage (KBs)	30,336	30,336	128	128
Total (KBs)	54,656	35,584	22,272	4864

Table 1.1 *Test Results with Small LOBs*

this table by more than compression alone did in DB2 9.5. Now the real magic happens: since the inlined LOBs are now compressible you can mix these features together, resulting in a sample table that has been reduced in this example by around 90 percent!

Usage Recommendations

As you can see, LOB inlining is so useful that DB2 intelligently does some of it on its own. For your own tables, we recommend that you consider inlining LOBs that are small enough to fit entirely on a data page, frequently accessed, and compressible. As you explicitly enable LOB inlining, keep in mind that your tables are obviously going to grow because the LOB data is moved into the base table (overall database size will decrease, however), making the industry-leading DB2 compression a perfect compliment to this technology.

Say Goodbye to the High Water Mark: New Table Space Storage Type

DB2 9.7 introduces a more flexible table space storage type that can help reduce storage usage. The DB2 9.7 documentation refers to this new storage type as *reclaimable storage table spaces*; however, we think this is a bit of a misnomer because it implies that without this storage type, table spaces don't allow for storage reclamation. This is, of course, is not the case as you can reclaim space from table spaces prior to DB2 9.7 in many ways. The key advantage of the new table space type is that you can reclaim storage that is embedded within the table space that was previously difficult to reclaim.

Perhaps the best way to describe this new table space type is through illustration. Assume a table space called TS1 contains five tables (T1, T2, T3, T4,

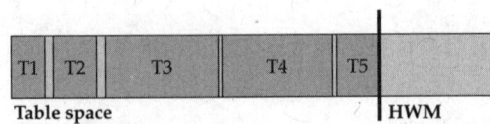

Figure 1.2 *Table space with five tables*

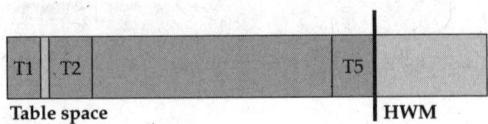

Figure 1.3 *Embedded free space*

and T5) as shown in Figure 1-2. You can see that in Figure 1-2 a lot of the space in this table space has been allocated to these tables and that the high water mark (HWM) for the table space is at the high end of the table space.

Now assume that tables T3 and T4 are dropped, as shown in Figure 1-3. It would not be possible to use the ALTER TABLESPACE REDUCE command to free up the embedded free space within the table space because table T5 is holding up the HWM, which cannot in this example be lowered or moved.

Prior to DB2 9.7, one possible solution would be to run the REORG command offline on table T5 which would create a duplicate copy of the T5 table earlier in the table space map. This would effectively move T5 down the table space and make the free space all contiguous at the high end of the table space. At this point, it would be possible to reduce the size of the table space and free up that storage to the operating system.

With DB2 9.7 this problem disappears. The new table space type allows DB2 to move T5 down the table space using the ALTER TABLESPACE tablespace_name LOWER HIGH WATER MARK command. In this example, this command would move table T5 down to the lower end of the table space and move the HWM down as low as possible, as shown in Figure 1-4. This is accomplished by moving the extents of T5 down to free extents at the lower end of the table space. This enables you to reduce the size of the table space and free up the unused storage back to the operating system, as shown in Figure 1-4.

While the LOWER HIGH WATER MARK option is in progress and table extents are being moved, you can monitor the progress using the MON_GET_EXTENT_MOVEMENT_STATUS new monitor table function, which

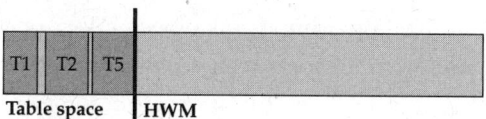

Figure 1.4 *Compacted table space*

will provide the number of extents moved, the number of extents remaining to move, and the time taken to move these extents.

The new table space type that this feature relies on is the default for any newly created DMS or Automatic Storage (which is based on the DMS infrastructure) table space in DB2 9.7. The next logical question is how to convert an existing table space in a database that was upgraded to DB2 9.7 from the previous storage type to the new reclaimable storage type. No automatic conversion capability is available in DB2 9.7 to do this for you. You must move your tables into a new table space created with this new storage mechanism. To do this, first create a new table space after you upgrade to DB2 9.7. Then, move your tables from the older table space to the new table space. We recommend that you leverage the new DB2 9.7 online table move feature so that you can convert to the new table space type online and without impacting your production system. After you have moved all your tables over to the new table space, you can drop the previous table space, which would now be empty.

If you want to check which table spaces in your DB2 9.7 database are using the new storage type and which ones are using the old storage type, use the MON_GET_TABLESPACE table function. The RECLAIMABLE_SPACE_ENABLED column will show 1 if the table space is using the new storage type and 0 otherwise.

Sparse Multidimensional Clustering Tables

A multidimensional clustering (MDC) table is an object, unique to DB2, that provides enormous performance gains for dimensionally organized schemas (such as a star schema) that are typically found in business intelligence (BI) applications. Although delving into the details and benefits of MDC tables is outside the scope of this book (MDCs have been around since DB2 8), they are potentially the most important schema object you will ever create in your BI database. We strongly recommend that you get to know this object and make plans to implement it within your warehouse. In fact, MDC tables are so powerful that SAP builds its star schema within its SAP Business Information

Warehouse (BW) application around this object. *eWeek* once reviewed MDC tables and "saw a performance improvement as much as 40% when performing multidimensional queries," and this was before some of the enhancements in the DB2 9 versions.

Why do SAP and other clients "in the know" love MDC tables?

- A DBA doesn't have to create any dimensional indexes on these tables; DB2 *automatically creates and manages* an MDC table's dimensional indexes for you.

- A DBA *never defragments* an MDC table for reclustering. The only time a DBA would reorganize an MDC table is to perform space reclamation, and that can be done online as of DB2 9.7 (this is the new enhancement to MDC tables that we talk about in this chapter).

- *MDC dimensional indexes are naturally compressed by about 95 percent* when compared to their RID-based counterparts, because MDC index pointers are coarsified to the page level, as opposed to the row level like their RID index counterparts. Note that you can mix MDC indexes with traditional RID indexes and benefit from the new index compression algorithms detailed earlier in this chapter.

- MDC tables allow you to have up to *64 clustered indexes* on a single table. Normal table structures (in DB2 and in other databases) limit you to a single clustering key for a table.

- MDC tables *perform optimized disk I/O* because of their patented disk allocation method. In a world where I/O is the limiting factor for high-scale data warehousing performance, this is a major benefit in addition to other technologies (such as hash partitioning and compression) offered by DB2.

- MDCs tables are *full compliments to other DB2 technologies* such as table partitioning, compression, and more.

The MDC Table Enhancement Train

MDC tables were first introduced in DB2 8. Since their inception, they've been continually enhanced to provide more and more benefits to the databases that implement them.

For example, in the DB2 8.2 release, the Design Advisor was extended to support MDC tables for optimal dimension selection based on your query workload. In DB2 8.2.2, rolled-out record data was optionally achieved in a highly optimized fashion because the roll-out algorithm could be performed on a page-by-page basis with drastically reduced logging, compared to the then default row-by-row mechanism. In DB2 9, this optional roll-out algorithm was hardened as the new default. In DB2 9.5, the interaction between MDC tables and secondary RID indexes was optimized via a new optional asynchronous secondary cleanup algorithm. Essentially, the record-by-record cleanup processing for deleted data could occur in a nonblocking manner behind the scenes, *but* DB2 was smart enough to know the record was deleted during scans and so on. The cumulative effect of these MDC optimizations has resulted in observed performance boosts of 50 to 90 percent (depending on the workload) when compared to the initial technology introduced in DB2 8.

Bottom line: With the kinds of investments IBM has been making in MDC tables in its new releases, you really need to get on the MDC train. The good news is that DB2 9.7 includes yet another optimization that should make MDCs even more compelling. (As of DB2 9.7, MDC tables can also house pureXML column data; this topic is discussed in Chapter 5.)

Storage Reclamation and MDC Tables Prior to DB2 9.7

At this point, you might want to run out and get an MDC tattoo. So what's wrong with MDC tables prior to DB2 9.7? Nothing, really; however, there was a storage nit that a DBA or two could justifiably comment about when rolling out a lot of data. Specifically, the space made available within the table after a data roll-out operation could be used only by the table and not by other tables (or objects) within the same table space, as illustrated in Figure 1-5.

In Figure 1-5, you can see the data for the 2004 and NW dimensions have been rolled out of the table. On the right side of this figure, you can see that the space occupied by this dimensional set is still under the control of the MDC table.

So what's the problem? Imagine a scenario where you had a massive roll-out of data but experienced a table space full condition for other tables in the same table space, even though there was all this empty space in the MDC table. Of course, this unused space is transparently reusable by the MDC table. For example, let's say another transaction inserted data that belonged to the 2004 and

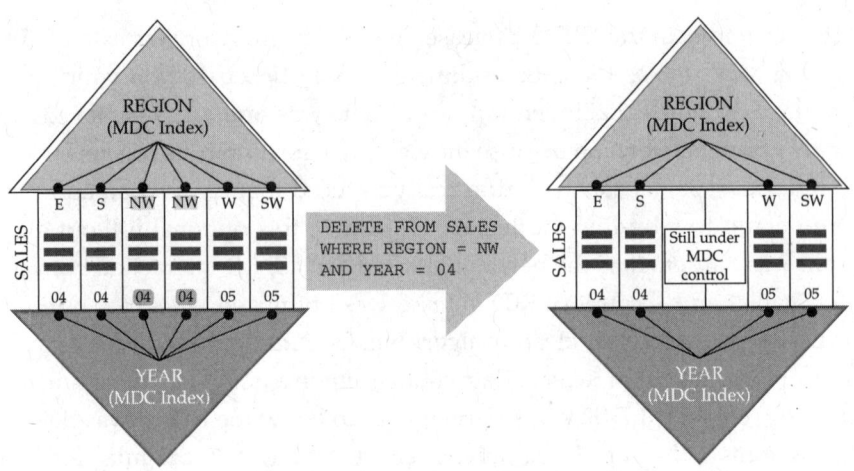

Figure 1.5 *Freed space in an MDC table still belongs to the MDC table in DB2 9.5.*

E dimensional set—this data would be inserted into the MDC table and could leverage this empty space (that's why we referred to it as a *nit*—if you're always rolling in and out data from your MDC table, this isn't an issue). The nit is that before DB2 9.7, the only way to return this unused space to the table space was to do a classic REORG. To solve this problem in releases prior DB2 9.7, the classic REORG had to reconstruct the table object and then truncate any free space that was no longer needed: as you can imagine, this was a time-consuming process since it didn't allow concurrent write activities to the table.

Reclaiming Storage from MDC Tables in DB2 9.7

While the free space shown in Figure 1-5 is still available for reuse by the MDC table, in some cases, you may want to use that space for another table that resides in the same table space as the MDC table you just deleted data from. To avoid having to take this table offline, DB2 9.7 introduces the RECLAIM EXTENTS ONLY extension to the REORG command (you can use this with the ALLOW WRITE, READ, and NO options). This extension allows you to free the unused space back to the table space without having to take an outage. After running this command, the space in Figure 1-5 can be used by any table in the table space.

The truth of the matter is that this isn't really a REORG at all (no shadow copy of the table is created, no copy phase, and so on), which is a great because this means it's going to run blazingly fast. A RECLAIM EXTENTS ONLY reorganization finds the newly emptied block in the MDC table's block map, marks those blocks as unallocated (now the MDC table no longer thinks the empty blocks belong to it), and then marks block as unallocated in the table space storage map (now the table space thinks it can use them).

DB2 9.7 even added a new column (called RECLAIMABLE_SPACE) to the result set of the ADMIN_GET_TAB_INFO() function, which gives you a good idea of when it may be beneficial to reorganize an MDC table with the RECLAIM EXTENTS ONLY option. For example, if you wanted to see all the MDC tables that had potentially reclaimable space greater than 10MB, you could use the following command:

```
SELECT TABSCHEMA, TABNAME, RECLAIMABLE_SPACE FROM
SYSIBMADM.ADMINTABLEINFO WHERE RECLAIMABLE_SPACE >
10,000,000 GROUP BY TABSCHEMA, TABNAME
```

If you wanted to get this data for a specific table, you could use something similar to the following:

```
SELECT RECLAIMABLE_SPACE FROM TABLE
  (SYSPROC.ADMIN_GET_TAB_INFO_V97('PAULZ', 'T1'))"
```

Furthermore, you could use a WHERE clause to return a value only if it exceeded a specified size.

Finally, since MDC tables have an ease-of-use culture, you can have your automated table maintenance policy invoke a REORG with the RECLAIM EXTENTS ONLY clause so you don't even have to get involved!

We didn't mention that as a by-product to all this efficiency, your MDC table performance can get even faster! For example, prior to DB2 9.7, perhaps the optimizer may have chosen to sequentially prefetch some of the data. In this case, it could actually have been fetching empty blocks in to the buffer since they were attached to a dimension within the MDC table. So now the optimizer may avoid fetching these pages altogether and worse yet, pushing out victim pages with pages that are full of data!

Bottom line is this: DB2 9.7 gives you even more reasons to get on the MDC train and ride it to the land of performance and automation (a great destination in our humble opinion).

2

The Even More Manageable DB2

Since the DB2 8.2 release (when *eWeek* gave DB2 Administration a rating of "Excellent" and SQL Server 2005 "Good"), an incredible number of automation features have been driven into the product. Truly, DB2 8.2 was an inflection point for ease of use, and the subsequent DB2 9 and DB2 9.5 releases created an unstoppable inertia with the introduction of Self Tuning Memory Manager (STMM), a threaded memory model, a significant number of parameters that can be set to AUTOMATIC, and more. DB2 9.7 continues this momentum and delivers a number of time-saving features such as online table move, relaxed schema evolution, local partitioned indexes, and more, that might just let you head out the door a little earlier on Fridays.

> **NOTE:** In this chapter we talk a lot about some really cool schema evolution and performance monitoring features in DB2 9.7. The IBM Optim Solutions portfolio—for example, Optim Database Administrator—can help automate these tasks and provide even more value.

Online Table Move

A great new feature of DB2 9.7 is the ability to move a table online. Using online table move, you can move the data in a table to another table of the same name that has potentially different storage characteristics and other DBA tasks; you can think of an online table move as a DBA's "jackknife." During this operation, the source table remains accessible for all Data Manipulation Language (DML) operations (SELECT, INSERT, UPDATE, and DELETE). The table is offline only for a short period at the end of the operation, when the system tables are being updated to rename the target table (to the original table name).

So why use an online table move? There's no denying that it will always be more efficient, for those who can afford it, to perform this kind of maintenance offline, since an offline move will require less space, experience faster move performance, and have zero transaction overhead to contend with. However, for many of us, taking a table offline for maintenance is just not possible in today's IT climate: critical tables must stay accessible and available all the time.

With the real world in mind, DB2 9.7's online table move is the way to go for those who need to make changes to a table, but can't afford the downtime. It can be used to move a table to a different table space; to change table characteristics such as adding or removing columns, changing column data types, or changing the order of a column; to add or change dimensions in a multidimensional clustering (MDC) table; to change table partitioning keys or partitioning ranges; to perform online table compression; to perform an online REORG or REDISTRIBUTE; to perform an online conversion to the LARGE table space format; and more (we were getting too tired to finish this list). All while keeping the table online and available!

How It Works

To move a table online, you use the new ADMIN_MOVE_TABLE stored procedure. In addition to the table and its data, the following objects are also transferred to the new table: views, triggers, indexes, constraints, security privileges, and table metadata. An online table move operation involves three tables: the *source table* (that stays online), the *target table*, and a *temporary staging table*. The staging table stores changes (INSERTs, UPDATEs, and DELETEs) that occur on the source table during the execution of the online move operation. The staging table is always created in the same table space as the target table, as well as with the same partitioning specification if it's a partitioned database. The staging table is dropped when the move is complete.

In DB2 9.7, online table move takes place in five distinct phases: INIT, COPY, REPLAY, SWAP, and CLEANUP. The INIT phase ensures that a table move can take place and initializes all of the objects (triggers, target table, and staging table) necessary in order to complete the operation. In this phase, triggers are created on the source table and subsequently used to capture all changes to the source table's data and places this information in the staging table. The `COPY` phase creates a copy of the source table at the very beginning of this phase and inserts that data into the target table. By default, the copy is performed using an `INSERT FROM SELECT` operation and is therefore a logged operation. You can also use the `LOAD` utility in the `COPY` phase if you invoke an online table move using the `COPY_USE_LOAD` option. Any `INSERT`, `UPDATE`, and `DELETE` activities that occur on the source table during this phase are captured and stored in the staging table. The `REPLAY` phase copies the rows that have changed in the source table since the `COPY` phase began into the target table. These changed rows have been captured by triggers created on the source table. The `SWAP` phase performs the actual swap between the source table and the target table; part of this phase involves briefly taking the source table offline to perform the rename of the tables and indexes—this is a very fast operation. The `CLEANUP` phase drops all the temporary objects created by the stored procedure (triggers, staging table, and original table if the `KEEP` option was not set) to support the movement of the table and its underlying object.

A sixth, optional phase called `VERIFY` is mainly used for debugging purposes and will check to determine whether the contents of the new table and the source table are identical. The `VERIFY` phase can occur only after the `COPY` and `REPLAY` phases, as it involves obtaining a shared lock on the source and target tables, replaying any changes that have occurred on the source table, and then performing the comparison. Since this is an expensive operation that takes a shared lock on the source table, we don't recommended using it during a table move in a production environment (use it in your Q/A environment) unless you're certain it won't impact your service level agreement.

Before you attempt to move a table online, you should ensure that you've got sufficient disk space to accommodate the copies of the table and indexes, the staging table, and the additional log entries (for example, the `COPY` phase is a logged operation). You can cancel an online table move at any time and can control when the target table is taken offline to be updated.

You can invoke the `ADMIN_MOVE_TABLE` stored procedure in two ways:

- **Method 1 - The easy method**

    ```
    SYSPROC.ADMIN_MOVE_TABLE (IN TABSCHEMA, IN TABNAME,
    IN DATA_TBSP, IN  INDEX_TBSP, IN  LOB_TBSP, IN
    MDC_COLS, IN PARTKEY_COLS, IN RANGE_PART, IN COLDEF,
    IN OPTIONS, IN OPERATION)
    ```

- **Method 2 - More control and flexibility**

    ```
    SYSPROC.ADMIN_MOVE_TABLE (IN TABSCHEMA, IN TABNAME,
    IN TARGET_TABNAME, IN OPTIONS, IN OPERATION)
    ```

Both methods can be invoked in one call, so that it starts and finishes all the phases required for an online table move for you, or they can be alternatively executed multiple times on a phase-by-phase basis to control manually when each phase of the move occurs.

Which online table method you use depends on your needs. Although the first signature is longer, it is the simpler one to use. It allows you to modify the most common table definition attributes you want to change, without having to specify anything else. If you leave a parameter blank, the stored procedure will use the definition from the existing source table for that parameter. For example, if all you want to do is modify a table's table space you'd simply specify the `DATA_TBSP`, `INDEX_TBSP`, and `LOB_TBSP` parameters, and leave the other optional parameters blank:

```
CALL SYSPROC.ADMIN_MOVE_TABLE( 'TASSI', 'SOURCE',
'ACCOUNTING', 'ACCOUNTING', 'ACCOUNTING', '', '', '',
'','','MOVE');
```

Assuming the move was successful, a short report will be returned, indicating the times and summary details for each phase of the move.

The second method, in contrast, gives you more control and flexibility. Specifically, this method allows you to create the target table yourself before invoking the operation (rather than having the stored procedure do it for you). You can then pass in the newly created target table, via the `TARGET_TABNAME` parameter, and it will be used by the stored procedure. Specifying the target table manually using the granular method allows you, for example, to turn on row compression automatically as part of the move even if the source table didn't have row compression enabled. If this parameter is blank, the stored procedure will automatically create a target table as in method 1.

You initiate a one shot move, using either method, by passing `MOVE` into the `OPERATIONS` parameter. To perform the move in manual stages, you use the `OPERATIONS` parameter to specify the phase you want. It will accept the following values: `INIT`, `COPY`, `REPLAY`, `VERIFY`, or `SWAP`. You can also specify the `CLEANUP` option, but since this phase is called automatically by the `SWAP` phase, you're not likely to use it. When you invoke each phase manually, you have to call each phase in the order in which the automated method calls it. For example, you must invoke the `INIT` phase the first time you call the

`ADMIN_MOVE_TABLE` routine. If you wanted to move a table within its own table space while the table remains online using the granular method you would ultimately call `ADMIN_MOVE_TABLE` routine as follows:

```
CALL SYSPROC.ADMIN_MOVE_TABLE ('TASSI', 'SOURCE','','','INIT');
CALL SYSPROC.ADMIN_MOVE_TABLE ('TASSI', 'SOURCE','','','COPY');
CALL SYSPROC.ADMIN_MOVE_TABLE ('TASSI', 'SOURCE','','','REPLAY');
CALL SYSPROC.ADMIN_MOVE_TABLE ('TASSI', 'SOURCE','','','SWAP');
```

Although this procedure should be called in this order, the phases do not have to run one immediately after the other. For example, you can wait until an appropriate time of the day to initiate the SWAP phase and its associated short offline period.

You can determine the current stage of an ongoing online table move operation by querying the SYSTOOLS.ADMIN_MOVE_TABLE table. If this table query returns a status that's anything other than COMPLETED or CLEANUP, you can cancel the move by specifying the CANCEL option when invoking the routine again.

Things to Consider When Performing an Online Table Move

When deciding whether or not to perform an online table move, keep the following in mind:

- You must have enough disk and log space (since online table move is a logged operation) for a full copy of the table and all of its indexes, as well as the space needed for the shadow copy table.

- Foreign keys (child or parent) can't be defined on the source table. If you want to move a table with foreign keys, we recommend that you capture these business rules using DB2LOOK, drop them from the table, perform the move operation, and then re-create them.

- Unique or primary indexes are required if XML or large object (LOB) columns are present; we recommend this as a best practice for efficiency reasons anyway, but it's a requirement for online table move operations involving these data types. Performing an online move for a table without any unique indexes might result in a complex or expensive REPLAY phase, so this is not recommended for production table moves.

- The source table must be a simple regular table: Materialized Query Tables (MQTs), typed tables, system tables, views, and so on, are not supported by this utility. Refer to the DB2 9.7 Information Center for more details.

Transportable Schemas

Transportable schemas are an exciting new feature that will slash the administration times associated with your DB2 table spaces. Another vendor in the industry calls this feature "transportable table space," but we like to think that transportable schemas encompass this feature and more!

NOTE: *Transportable schemas slipped out of the general availability release of DB2 9.7, but the development labs are working on the technology to deliver it as soon as possible (likely in an up-and-coming Fix Pack).*

Bottom line: When this feature is delivered, DB2 9.7 will contain an exciting new capability to let you move schemas and table spaces easily between databases, with *no impact* to the source systems.

Transportable schemas allows you to quickly move many of the important physical and logical objects a schema contains, as well as the data from a source backup image to a target database. The schema objects that will be moved include the tables, indexes, views, user-defined types (UDTs), MQTs, statistics, constraints, functions, privileges, packages, and more. As you can likely tell, transportable schemas have a multitude of valuable use cases including the ability to quickly create a fast test system from a production backup image.

The source objects to be moved can be specified as one or more schemas from one or multiple table spaces. The target of this move can be any DB2 database on the same hardware architecture and operating system as the source; basically the transportability of objects follows the same rules for BACKUP and RESTORE operations. (It really comes down to compatibility of the Endian encoding schema across platforms, so in some cases, you can do this across operating systems.) Note, however, that the target database can have different page sizes, containers, or database storage paths from the source backup, which are also great use cases for this new feature. The transportable schema feature won't be supported in DB2 9.7 for DB2 Database Partitioning Feature (DPF) environments when it first becomes available for DB2 users.

NOTE: *If the source backup used for transportable schemas was an online backup, the target database must be at the same version level as DB2. If the source for the schema movement was an offline backup, you can move the schema objects to a database that is up to two versions down-level from the backup image.*

How Transportable Schemas Work

Transportable schemas are essentially redirected restore operations that work across databases at a schema-level granularity. The source schemas can be wholly contained in a single table space or spread out across multiple table spaces. The only thing you need to ensure is that the set of schemas and table spaces (called a *transport set*) you are moving are self contained: you can't move parts of a schema. Figure 2-1 shows some examples of what is and isn't considered a transport set. The first two examples are valid transport sets since the schemas are fully contained in the table spaces that are moving. In contrast, the third example would not be a valid transport set (the dashed rounded rectangle)—to make it work, you would need to bring schema5 and tablespace6 along for the "ride" (the solid-lined rounded rectangle). See the DB2 9.7 Information Center for details.

Once initialized, a transport goes through the following steps:

1. Restores the SYSCATSPACE and specified table spaces from the backup image.
2. Rolls forward involved to a consistant point in time (PIT).
3. Validates the schemas that you specified for transport.

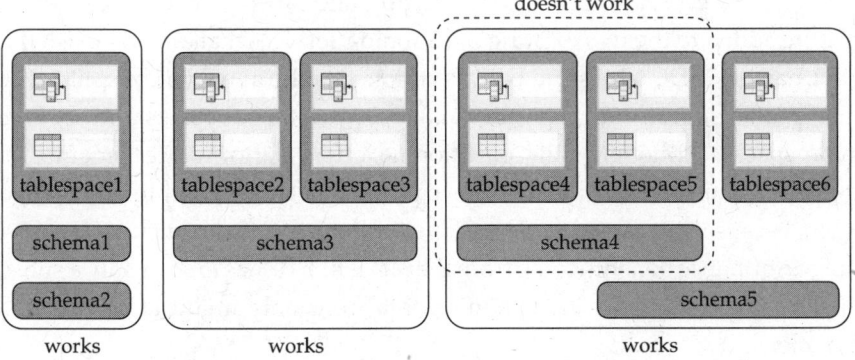

Figure 2.1 *An example of different scenarios that are and aren't supported with transportable schemas*

4. Transfers ownership of the specified table spaces to the target database.
5. Re-creates the schema in the target database.

Under the covers, transportable schema uses a small staging database mainly consisting of the system catalog table space from the backup image. By default, this supporting temporary database will be created in the DFTDBPATH as part of the move operation. This database will be automatically dropped once the utility completes the transport request. Alternatively, you can specify your own database name and location for this staging database, but it'll be up to you to drop it afterward.

Transportable Schemas: A Simple Example

Assume we wanted to create a new test database that initially contains two schemas, TASSI and MCINNIS, that we want to move from a production backup image to set up a test database. Both schemas are fully contained in one table space called TBLSP1, which is wholly contained within this backup image. To create a new database and perform the transport schema move, we would simply enter the following commands:

```
CREATE DATABASE testdb AUTOMATIC STORAGE YES ON C: DBPATH ON D:;
RESTORE DB productiondb TABLESPACE ('tblsp1') SCHEMA ('tassi',
'mcinnis') TRANSPORT INTO testdb;
```

It's that easy! Our new test database is ready with two simple commands!

Table Partitioning Enhancements

DB2 9 delivered a new form of data partitioning called *partitioned tables*. This feature added to the two existing partitioning services that already existed in DB2, namely MDC tables and DPF. Partitioned tables allow you to split a table into smaller subsets (or ranges of data) and place those subsets into separate table spaces. Although table partitioning offers performance benefits, we think that main benefit of being able to partition a table is simplified management, because you can add and remove portions of a table quickly. Of course the performance benefits come from the fact that DB2 has to scan only a subset of the table for queries that require data from only a subset of the table partitions.

The following is an example of a table that is partitioned by month and stored in five separate table spaces (one for each month of data):

```
CREATE TABLE orders
(
    orderkey       DECIMAL(10,0) NOT NULL,
    orderdate      DATE,
    price          DECIMAL(12,2),
    status         CHAR(1)
)
IN  tablespace1, tablespace2,
tablespace3, tablespace4, tablespace5
PARTITION BY RANGE(orderdate)
(STARTING '1/1/2009' ENDING '5/31/2009' EVERY 1 MONTH)
```

In this example, data in the ORDERS table that had an ORDERDATE of January 2009 would be stored in `tablespace1`, February in `tablespace2`, and so on, to May data in `tablespace5`.

In DB2 9 and DB2 9.5, any index created on a partitioned table is known as a *global index*. That is, all keys and ROWIDs for all rows in all table partitions for a given table would be stored in a *single* index object—even though the data was stored in multiple index objects. For example, the following index on the previously defined ORDERS table would have index keys for all five months' worth of data and would therefore be considered a global index:

```
CREATE INDEX order_key_index ON orders(orderkey)
```

The ORDER_KEY_INDEX global index is very useful in transactional systems since you can use a global index to ensure the uniqueness of the key values. Although DB2 can enforce uniqueness using a unique index, DB2 would have to check to ensure that any new keys that are added aren't duplicates of any existing keys during processing. In contrast, with a partitioned table's global index, DB2 can efficiently check for duplicate values during row insert processing, because it doesn't matter in which partition the data resides, since all keys are stored in a single global index object.

With that said, some disadvantages are associated with using global indexes. For example, if you want to drop a range of data from an existing partitioned table, DB2 would have to go into the global index and remove all those keys from the deleted date range. If you wanted to roll out our example's January 2009 data, DB2 would have to go into the global ORDER_KEY_INDEX index and find all the keys that point to January rows and remove them from the index. This can take some time and consume a large amount of log space if the data partition is large. To mitigate this processing, DB2 has asynchronous index cleanup processing for partitioned tables, so DB2 deletes these index keys efficiently in the background. Similarly, if you added a large amount of data by attaching a new data partition, DB2 would have to add all these new index keys to the global index. Again this can take some time (as it is performed as part of the SET INTEGRITY command on the table *after* the ATTACH command) and can also consume a large amount of log space.

DB2 9.7 Extends Table Partitioning with Partitioned Index Support

DB2 9.7 helps alleviate the aforementioned issues associated with global indexes on partitioned tables by introducing *local partitioned index* support for partitioned tables. Partitioned indexes (often called *local indexes*) allow for a single index to be partitioned in the same manner as the underlying table. Continuing with this chapter's example of the ORDER_KEY_INDEX index on the ORDERS table, the syntax to create a partitioned index is simply to add the PARTITIONED clause as part of the CREATE INDEX statement, as follows:

```
CREATE INDEX order_key_index ON orders(orderkey) PARTITIONED
```

By default, as of DB2 9.7, if you create a partitioned table, any index created on that table will be partitioned (a local index) *even* if the PARTITIONED keyword is not specified. (There are some exceptions to this, but they are outside the scope of this book.) To create a global index on a partitioned table in DB2 9.7, you must use the NONPARTITIONED keyword on the CREATE INDEX statement. In the example shown in Figure 2-2, all the row keys for each month's data will be contained in the local indexes associated with that month.

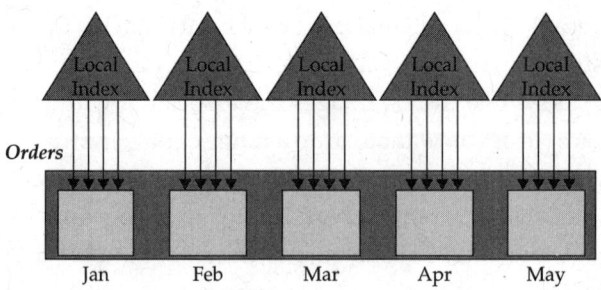

Figure 2.2 *DB2 9.7 local indexes allow DB2 to have a specific index for a specific range in a partitioned table.*

Similarly, all keys for February data will be contained in the February local index partition, and so on.

Table Spaces for Partitioned Indexes

By default, a partitioned index is stored in the *same* table space as the data to which the index keys are pointing. For example, the working example in this chapter has the ORDERS table spread across five table spaces (one for each month); the default behavior for a partitioned index on this table would be for the index keys pointing to January rows to be stored in `tablespace1`, while index keys pointing to rows for February would be stored in `tablespace2`, and so on.

If you want to have partitioned indexes stored in different table spaces than the default behavior, you *must* specify the partitioned index storage locations as part of the `CREATE TABLE` statement using the `INDEX IN` clause on the individual partition clauses of the `CREATE TABLE` command. For example, the following command creates a partitioned table whose partitioned indexes are stored in separate table spaces from the row partitions:

```
CREATE TABLE orders
(
       orderkey       DECIMAL(10,0) NOT NULL,
       orderdate      DATE,
       price          DECIMAL(12,2),
       status         CHAR(1)
)
IN   tablespace1, tablespace2,
tablespace3, tablespace4, tablespace5
PARTITION BY RANGE(orderdate)
(STARTING '1/1/2009' ENDING '5/31/2009' INDEX IN index_space1,
 STARTING '2/1/2009' ENDING '2/28/2009' INDEX IN index_space2,
 STARTING '3/1/2009' ENDING '3/31/2009' INDEX IN index_space3,
 STARTING '4/1/2009' ENDING '4/30/2009' INDEX IN index_space4,
 STARTING '5/1/2009' ENDING '5/31/2009' INDEX IN index_space5)
```

Note that all partitioned indexes on the ORDERS table will be stored in these index table spaces. Any nonpartitioned indexes can be stored in any table space you want by using the `IN TABLESPACE` clause of the `CREATE INDEX` command. If you are creating a partitioned index, you can't specify the `IN TABLESPACE` option on the `CREATE INDEX` command (the index is stored in the location specified by the `CREATE TABLE` command).

Unique Indexes

You have two choices for unique indexes on partitioned tables. First, you can use a global unique index (known also as a *nonpartitioned global unique index*). As in previous releases, global indexes can be defined as either unique or non-unique. To create a unique partitioned index in DB2 9.7, the index definition *must* be a superset of the table partitioning key. In this chapter's example, to define a unique index on the partitioned ORDERS table, that index *must* include the ORDERDATE column as its table partitioning key. By doing this, DB2 will be able to enforce uniqueness of the index since all the values in the index for a given ORDERDATE will reside in the same index partition.

DB2 9.7 Makes Rolling in and out Data Fast

As discussed earlier in this chapter, one of the disadvantages of global indexes is the time and resources required to create and delete the key values during ATTACH and DETACH processing. This is where local indexes can really show their strength. When a table partition is detached, the data is "moved" into its own standalone table. Similarly, if you have partitioned indexes, they are "moved" out of the partitioned index object (in the same mannner that partitioned tables are part of a single table object; partitioned indexes are part of a single index object) to become a standalone index on the newly detached table object. Figure 2-3 illustrates what happens if you detach the January partition of the ORDERS table.

As you can see Figure 2-3, the ORDER_KEY_INDEX index on that January partition is removed from the partitioned index and now becomes a simple standalone index on the JANUARY table. This DETACH processing requires minimal logging, and you can then optionally drop the January index and the

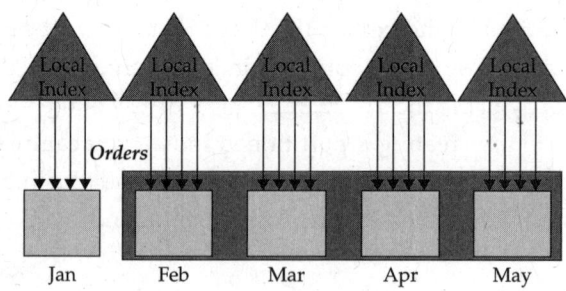

Figure 2.3 *Detaching a partition with a local index*

associated local index as well with minimal logging and resource consumption. There is no need for asynchronous index cleanup in this case.

Similarly, if you want to attach a new partition, you simply need to create an index on the table data that you want to attach, and then use the `ALTER TABLE ATTACH` command to add the new data partition and associated index partition. Again, in this example, there is no global index to maintain and therefore logging is kept to a minimum and the time taken to attach the new partition can be greatly reduced. Figure 2-4 demonstrates the steps involved in attaching a new partition with a local index.

Note that if you attach a data partition without first creating local indexes, DB2 will create these partitioned indexes as part of the `ATTACH` process on your behalf. Also, note that a partitioned table can have *both* partitioned and non-partitioned indexes on it. Therefore, the `ATTACH` process will create any missing partitioned indexes and also maintain any global indexes that exist on a table as part of the `SET INTEGRITY` command after the `ATTACH` completes.

Utility Support for Partitioned Tables

As of the time this book was written, technology currently under development (we're guessing it will be delivered in an up and coming Fix Pack) will allow you to run the `REORG` command on individual data partitions. This benefits DBAs because it means they would be able to reorganize only a single data partition and/or a single index partition of a larger table. This flexibility would be extremely useful in conjunction with DB2's compression capabilities.

For example, assume you added a new data partition for the current month's data (and associated local indexes). As the business transacts, new

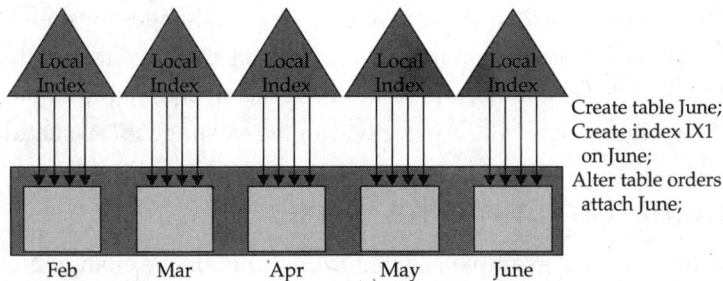

Figure 2.4 *Attaching a new partition with a local index is faster*

rows are added to the table's most current data partition. Once the partition has sufficient data in it, DB2's automatic dictionary creation (ADC) kicks in and creates a compression dictionary for this new partition, and any further data added is automatically compressed. At the end of the month, you could reorganize this single partition to create a new and more optimized compression dictionary that would give you dynamic optimal compression for this partition without having to modify any data in any of the other table partitions.

Schema Evolution

In today's production landscape, database systems generally have well-defined schemas, and most companies employ some form of change-control process to ensure that any changes that need to take place do so in an orderly and well-tested manner to avoid instability. However, many application developers and those who work with applications purchased from third parties find it necessary to change the database schema as they develop new functionality into their applications. (Flexibility is a driver of the ever-increasing interest in XML as a data store, and we cover this in Chapter 5.) For example, an application may have customer numbers built into the database as integers since the initial application assigned integer values to customers who registered with the company. However, some bright application developer decided that the addition of an alphabetic character into a customer number would be useful for some reason—or at least it would make those unique identifiers prettier. The by-product of this application change means that when the new version of the application is deployed, the tables that contain customer numbers must be changed to accommodate alphabetic characters rather than just integers, And, of course, in today's connected world, everything must happen online.

DB2 has been focused on allowing online schema changes for some time. In DB2 9.7, many of the evolutionary schema changes that used to require a brief outage can now occur online, and some changes that once required the re-creation of the table can now take place within the existing table structure.

Changing Column Data Types

As described, a good example of schema evolution is the changing of a column's data type. Although it's less typical to change from an integer data type to a character, it's not uncommon to change the size of a column. For example, you may want to increase the size of a character string (which DB2 has been able to do online and in-place for some time). Other changes are more difficult, such as changing a character to an integer or a decimal to a character string. However, as of DB2 9.7, any data type changes that you can do using the CAST function in SQL can now be done natively using the ALTER TABLE table_name and ALTER COLUMN col_name SET DATA TYPE commands. For example, in DB2 9.7 it's possible to cast an INTEGER column to a FLOAT and vice-versa, or you can change a CHARACTER column to an INTEGER and vice-versa. Almost all combinations are possible in DB2 9.7. You can even shrink the size of a character column, assuming the truncated data in the column is padded with blank characters.

As part of the ALTER COLUMN SET DATA TYPE command, DB2 will perform a full scan on the column (assuming it's not a simple and obviously safe operation such as increasing the size of the column type). As part of this column scan, DB2 will check to ensure that the required data type change does not result in an overflow (for example, converting a BIGINT to an INTEGER where data in the column would become larger than an integer type can hold), truncation (where a column contains character data larger than the new column type can hold), or an illegal conversion between data types (such as converting a character type to integer where some data in the column is not numeric). If any of these situations occur, DB2 will return a SQL0190 SQL error code, indicating that the conversion could not take place.

Other column changes, such as shrinking the size of a column and truncating non-blank characters, are also possible with DB2 9.7's online table move feature outlined earlier in this chapter.

Change Column Names in Real Time

DB2 9.7 also supports changing column names within a base table. This is supported with a new ALTER TABLE command option as follows:

ALTER TABLE table_name RENAME COLUMN source_name TO target_name

When you run this command, DB2 will rename the column in the table and invalidate any objects (such as views) that are dependant on this column in this table. Dependant objects will be revalidated immediately if possible.

Relax Object Dependencies Including Automatic Revalidation

Prior to DB2 9.7, in many cases, a schema change would invalidate an object that depends on the object being changed. This invalidation would force a DBA to drop that dependant object and re-create it. For example, a view created on top of a table could become invalidated if a column used by that view was dropped from the base table. In such an event, a DBA would have to drop the view and re-create it, *and then* regrant all of the privileges to the view. As you can imagine, this could be quite cumbersome and required careful planning of the schema change operation to ensure that all dependant objects were re-created appropriately.

DB2 9.7 has a much more relaxed and automated model for these types of dependent objects. In almost all cases, you can now have the dependant objects revalidated (effectively recreated) immediately or you can defer the revalidation to the first time a user accesses the dependant objects. This automatic and immediate revalidation is under the control of a new database configuration parameter called AUTO_REVAL. The default for this configuration parameter for new databases is DEFERRED, which means that all dependant objects that become invalidated due to a schema change will be automatically revalidated the next time the object is accessed. For databases that are upgraded from DB2 9.5 or previous releases, the default value for this configuration parameter is DISABLED, which offers the same behavior as in prior releases. We recommend that you change this parameter to achieve this efficient behavior after upgrading to DB2 9.7. A third possible value for this parameter is IMMEDIATE, which means that dependant objects will be automatically revalidated whenever the invalidation occurs. For example, if you alter a column's data type and AUTO_REVAL is set to IMMEDIATE, then any views on top of this altered table will automatically be revalidated and have the corresponding data type in the view changed.

Note that if you set this value either to DEFERRED or IMMEDIATE, if the revalidation of the dependant objects fails, the dependant objects will remain in an invalid state until they are accessed again. At that time, additional automatic revalidation attempts will be made. For example, if your database is set for IMMEDIATE revalidation, and you drop a table, but a view is defined on this table, that view will be invalidated and an attempt to revalidate that view will be made immediately. This revalidation will fail because the table that the view depends on doesn't exist. This view will remain invalid, and when the next user tries to access the view, another automatic revalidation will take place.

Finally, a fourth value is available for the AUTO_REVAL configuration parameter called DEFERRED_FORCE. This setting allows you to create objects that depend on other objects, even if the objects they depend on don't exist—that's cool! For example, if AUTO_REVAL is set to DEFERRED_FORCE, it would be possible to create a view on top of a table called T1 even if table T1 didn't exist.

To see what objects are currently invalid, you can query the SYSCAT. INVALIDOBJECTS catalog view. As mentioned, objects will immediately be revalidated (if available) or be revalidated as they are accessed. However, in some cases, you may want to revalidate invalid objects explicitly. DB2 9.7 delivers the new SYSPROC.ADMIN_REVALIDATE_DB_OBJECTS stored procedure that lets you validate invalid objects (either all of them at once or on a case-by-case basis). Here's an example of this new routine:

```
CALL SYSPROC.ADMIN_REVALIDATE_DB_OBJECTS(object_type,
object_schema, object_name)
```

Specifying a NULL value for this routine's parameters tells DB2 to treat that as a wildcard (*)—that is, all objects of that type, schema, or name. For example, if you specify NULL for all three parameters, that tells DB2 to revalidate every invalid object in the database. If you were to specify VIEW for object_type and NULL for both object_schema and object_name, then DB2 will revalidate all views in the database that are invalid.

New CREATE OR REPLACE Syntax for Objects

Another very useful new command in DB2 9.7 automatically performs invalidation of dependant objects while at the same time recreates the object and then revalidates the dependant object; it's called CREATE OR REPLACE. This command works on views, functions, procedures, triggers, aliases, nicknames, sequences, variables, and modules. The CREATE OR REPLACE command will create the specified object if it doesn't exist or drop the object, invalidate any dependant objects, and then re-create the object with the new definition if it already exists. (Quite simply, it effectively replaces the old object definition with a new one.) For dependant objects that can be immediately revalidated, DB2 will also revalidate those dependant objects.

For example, assume you have the following views defined:

```
CREATE VIEW v1 AS SELECT * FROM t1;
CREATE VIEW v2 AS SELECT * FROM v1;
```

In this case, it would be possible to run a CREATE OR REPLACE command as:

```
CREATE OR REPLACE v1 AS SELECT * FROM T2
```

This command would first invalidate the V2 view, then drop the V1 view, replace the V1 view with the new view definition (now it points to the T2 table instead of the T1 table), and finally immediately revalidate the V2 view.

Performance Monitoring Enhancements

With every release, the ability to zone in on performance "trouble spots" quickly and efficiently improves, and DB2 9.7 is no exception in this area. In fact, DB2 9.7 is likely the biggest release in terms of advancements in monitoring since it first shipped Event and Snapshot monitors. How so? DB2 is currently undergoing a shift in its internal monitoring infrastructure that will not only allow you to identify bottlenecks more quickly, but will also allow you to do this with the slightest impact possible. That is, you will be able to monitor the performance of applications, users, transactions, and so on *without* adding significantly to the resource utilization of the system. This has not been true of monitor elements in the past and is one of the main reasons that DB2 offered so many monitor switches in prior releases (to allow you to turn off the capture of some of the more costly to monitor metrics). Quite simply, a lot of engineering was put in place to minimize the impact of performance monitoring from a minimization of monitoring perspective, and that's now replaced in DB2 9.7 with maximizing the accessibility of this information with-in the new lightweight infrastructure perspective.

In this section, we talk about these new metrics and how DB2 is now capturing monitor elements more efficiently. We also talk about the infrastructure movement towards more *time spent metrics* rather than simple counters and how DB2 can more efficiently store and output monitor data.

New Performance Metrics with More Granularity

One of the greatest advances in DB2 monitoring is the increased focus on time spent metrics. That is, rather than focusing on the number of times an event took place, more emphasis is placed on the amount of time that was spent performing a task. That time is further broken down into two pieces: the amount of time DB2 spent doing something (sometimes referred to as the *component time*) and the amount of time DB2 spent waiting on something (such as waiting for an I/O or waiting on a lock).

By looking at the time spent doing work in DB2, and the time it spent waiting to be able to do that work, DBAs have a much easier time finding where the bottlenecks are in the system and can more easily resolve them. Both the component and the wait times are broken down at a granular level so you can see how DB2 is spending its time. For example, if you add up all the reported component time by category, you might find that DB2 is spending too much time compiling statements and too little time executing them, which is a leading indicator that you need to increase the package cache size. Perhaps you'll find by adding up the highest wait times that DB2 is spending too much time waiting on I/Os for a particular table or index, which is an indicator that not enough storage devices are behind that particular table or index.

In terms of granularity, DB2 9.7 lets you view monitor output at the system level, which can show you how much time it spent working in the buffer pool, performing commits, writing log records, compiling statements, and so on, for an entire system! In addition, you can look at data from an activity level that allows you to drill down into individual executing statements to see what's happening with individual query sections. Another way to look at the data is by object. For example, you may want to look at table or index data for a given object by drilling down from buffer pool activity into corresponding table space activity and then into individual table or index activities. Each of the aforementioned categories has a new monitor table function that can be easily called using an SQL statement to show you the details of any of these objects.

The first is *system-level monitoring*, which is available via a set of table functions are: `MON_GET_SERVICE_SUBCLASS`, `MON_GET_SERVICE_SUBCLASS_DETAILS`, `MON_GET_WORKLOAD`, `MON_GET_WORKLOAD_DETAILS`, `MON_GET_CONNECTION`, `MON_GET_CONNECTION_DETAILS`, `MON_GET_UNIT_OF_WORK`, `MON_GET_UNIT_OF_WORK_DETAILS`.

As you may notice, each table function also has a corresponding function of the same name with the added extension of `_DETAILS`. The shorter name version of the function returns the most common metrics in a column format, whereas the `_DETAILS` version returns all the metrics possible for that particular monitor in XML format. The shorter name version is more efficient as it does not require all monitor elements to be collected and displayed, whereas the `_DETAILS` version is more verbose and can therefore be used when you need to see those additional levels of detail.

The second function is the table function for *activity-level monitoring*. The `MON_GET_ACTIVITY_DETAILS` function retrieves a lot of information about a given statement in an XML format. For example, within this XML data are elements such as `TOTAL_CPU_TIME`, `TOTAL_ACT_TIME` (which is the total activity time for this statement), `TOTAL_WAIT_TIME` (which is the total time this statement has been waiting on something), and more. Within this XML output, you can also see the total activity time and total wait time broken down into component activity and component wait times, so you can find where DB2 is spending all its time.

The third facet is the set of *table functions for monitoring database objects*. These functions are `MON_GET_TABLE`, `MON_GET_INDEX`, `MON_GET_BUFFERPOOL`, `MON_GET_TABLESPACE`, and `MON_GET_CONTAINER`. Hopefully, their names are well representative of what each function reports. Although much of this information is available via SQL prior to DB2 9.7, the new monitor functions are more lightweight, as they pull relevant information *directly* from in-memory structures associated with the objects being monitored. Much like the other monitors already discussed, these table functions return the most commonly used metrics in a column format and also contain a column called `ADDITIONAL_DETAILS` that has an XML data stream containing a large number of other object metrics. In some cases, the `ADDITIONAL_DETAILS` column is not yet populated but is technology under development—but the framework is certainly there and the future of this area should be obvious.

Unformatted Event Table

Prior to DB2 9.7, event monitors could write their output to a file, a pipe, or a table. These output formats are useful in helping DBAs view the output of these monitors, because they are flexible and DB2 does all the work with the collected data to put them into a human-readable format. However, the process of formatting the data into a human-readable format and subsequently sending that data out of the database (either to a file or pipe) can be very costly and can impact system performance. In fact, if a lot of transactions are being captured by an event monitor, it's possible that the process of formatting and writing to a file or pipe could overwhelm the system and result in unacceptable levels of performance degradation. Storing the data in a DB2 table has an advantage in that the event monitor doesn't have to go outside the engine to store the information, but data formatting still adds overhead at record collection time. Finally, by storing the data in a regular table, some efficiencies aren't being utilized.

In DB2 9.7, you can store event monitor data in the new *unformatted event (UE) table*, which is optimized for storing monitor event data. By "optimized" we mean that the UE takes advantage of some DB2 features that allow for very fast insertion of data. Data is stored, as the name would suggest, in an unformatted binary large object (BLOB) column, and the data in the table is compressed (using DB2 compression internally, even if you're not licensed to use the Storage Optimization Feature). These optimizations allow DB2 to store more data in a more compact format and therefore give you more data to work with when viewing event monitor output. In addition, since the data is unformatted, there's a lot less overhead to the collection process, so even during peak workloads, the overhead of the event monitors is greatly reduced. In fact, the only overhead that occurs is the time it takes to format the records *when you want to view those records* (which may not be every record in the monitor table, so there is savings there as well). Finally, the formatter is even more efficient in DB2 9.7 (more on that in a bit).

The creation of the UE table is now part of the CREATE EVENT MONITOR command. Its syntax is shown here:

```
CREATE EVENT MONITOR monitor_name FOR event_type
WRITE TO UNFORMATTED EVENT TABLE
(TABLE table_name IN tablespace_name PCTDEACTIVATE pct)
```

Where the parameters are defined as follows:

- monitor_name is the name you specify to this event monitor.
- event_type is LOCKING, UOW, or PACKAGE CACHE STATEMENT, which are the three event monitors that currently support the UE table in DB2 9.7.
- table_name is the table you want to use to store the unformatted events.

- `tablespace_name` (optional) specifies the location of the UE table.
- `PCTDEACTIVEATE pct` tells DB2 that if the table space has reached the percentage specified by this parameter of storage used, then this event monitor should be automatically deactivated. The default setting for this parameter is `100`, which means that this the event monitor will automatically deactivate itself if the table space is 100 percent full. (This option is valid only if the UE table is directed to a DMS table space.)

Note that when this event monitor is created, DB2 will create the table for you with the name you specify as the UE table. If such a table already exists with the same name, and it is being used by another event monitor, then the `CREATE EVENT MONITOR` statement will fail, telling you that this table name is already in use. If no table name is specified, DB2 will use the `monitor_name` you specified as the name of the UE table. It's also important to know that if you drop the event monitor, its associated UE table *is not* dropped. This allows you to reuse that event table or keep it around to review the results later. You must *explicitly* drop the event table and you must also *explicitly* prune the contents of the event table if you want to remove any of the older data in the table.

Since event data can sometimes contain a large amount of data, we recommended that you store the unformatted event table in a table space that is using a 32KB page size. As mentioned, DB2 will try to store the event data as efficiently as possible, and as such it will use inline LOBs (see Chapter 1 for details on this great new DB2 9.7 feature) for the event data. Storing the data in a 32KB page size gives DB2 a greater ability to store the data inline with the row.

You should also note that the creation of an event monitor does not mean that event data will begin to be captured. The `CREATE EVENT MONITOR` statement only tells DB2 where and how to store the event data when it's collected. If you want to tell DB2 when to collect data and for whom it should be collected, you need to `CREATE` or `ALTER` a workload definition, which is discussed later in this chapter.

Viewing the Data in the Unformatted Event Table

Since the data in an UE table is in an unformatted BLOB and therefore unreadable to humans, DB2 9.7 provides three ways to view this data. The first is simply to produce a formatted text representation of the monitor data using a tool called `DB2EVMONFMT`. The second method lets you access the monitor data via

SQL using the new `EVMON_FORMAT_UE_TO_TABLES` stored procedure. This stored procedure outputs the event data as a set of relational tables that you can then query via SQL. The third option is available for those who want to build customized reports to view the monitor data; for these users, DB2 9.7 provides the new `EVMON_FORMAT_UE_TO_XML` stored procedure. Let's look at each of these in more detail.

The `DB2EVMONFMT` tool is located in the `sqllib/samples/java/jdbc` directory and uses a set of XSL Transformations (XLST) files (also located in this directory) that lets you format the output from the unformatted event table into a readable format. Furthermore, this tool gives you a fine-grained control that lets you focus on certain events that interest you, specific times that interest you, specific applications or users, and more. For details on the syntax of the tool and sample output, refer to the DB2 9.7 Information Center.

The `EVMON_FORMAT_UE_TO_XML` stored procedure call will read from the unformatted event table and output an XML representation of the event records that match your specification (time, applications, user, and so on). For example, if you want to view only the `LOCKWAIT` events from an UE table called `CEATON.MY_LOCK_EVENTS`, you would enter the following command:

```
SELECT formatted_lock.* FROM TABLE
    EVMON_FORMAT_UE_TO_XML (
       NULL,
       FOR EACH ROW OF (
         SELECT * FROM CEATON.MY_LOCK_EVENTS
           WHERE EVENT_TYPE='LOCKWAIT'
           ORDER BY EVENT_TIMESTAMP )) as formatted_lock;
```

The final UE data formatting option in DB2 9.7 lets you convert this data into a set of relational tables using a call to the `EVMON_FORMAT_UE_TO_TABLES` stored procedure. This procedure automatically creates a set of tables, then populates those tables using the `EVMON_FORMAT_UE_TO_XML` stored procedure, and finally shreds the XML output it receives from this routine into the target relational tables. Once this stored procedure is done processing, you can query the output tables using the SQL that best suits the reports you need to generate. You can pass several parameters as input into this stored procedure, and most of these parameters assume very logical default values, making it easy to call this routine. Here's an example:

```
CALL EVMON_FORMAT_UE_TO_TABLES( type, NULL, NULL, NULL, NULL,
NULL, NULL, commit_count, fullselect)
```

The NULLs tell DB2 to take the default for those parameters, so there are effectively only three parameters you need to worry about. The first is the event monitor type, which is either LOCKING or UOW. The second is the COMMIT_COUNT (it defaults to -1), which tells DB2 to commit after every 100 successful document decompositions into the target relational tables. (It can be set from 0, where it never commits until it's finished, to any number of records you want.) Finally the FULLSELECT statement is the same statement you would use to generate the XML in the preceding example. If you run this procedure using the LOCKING option, it will create the following additional tables: LOCK_EVENT, LOCK_PARTICIPANTS, LOCK_PARTICIPANT_ACTIVITIES, and LOCK_ACTIVITY_VALUES. The table created by the UOW event type is simply a table called UOW_EVENT.

Unit of Work (UOW) Event Monitor

As mentioned, the creation of an event monitor doesn't tell DB2 to start collecting event data; rather, you must create or alter the workload definition in order for DB2 to begin collecting event data. For example, the ALTER WORKLOAD WL1 COLLECT UNIT OF WORK DATA command will start the collection of UOW data for the workload defined by CHRIS_WORKLOAD and store that data in the UE table that was defined by the CREATE EVENT MONITOR statement. The way this is implemented in DB2 9.7 is great, because if you're using the DB2 Workload Manager (WLM) capabilities first introduced in DB2 9.5, you can isolate specific workloads and thereby capture UOW data only for those specific workloads of interest.

If you're looking for a simple way to capture UOW data, a new database configuration parameter in DB2 9.7 called MON_UOW_DATA can help; you can set this parameter dynamically so you don't have to recycle the database after changing it. This parameter can be set to NONE (the default), which tells DB2 not to collect any UOW event monitor data unless it's specifically asked for as part of the WLM workload definition. You can set MON_UOW_DATA=BASE, which tells DB2 to collect UOW data whenever a transaction commits or rolls back and then store this data in the UE event table defined by the CREATE EVENT MONITOR statement. You can get a plethora of output from a UOW event monitor, including time spent working in various portions of the DB2 engine, time spent waiting (on I/O, on locks, and so on), and more.

New Lock Event Monitor

While lots of engineering work went into DB2 9.7 to ensure that it acquires fewer locks and allows an even higher level of concurrency with the currently committed semantics (see Chapter 6 for more details), DB2 9.7 also delivers improved lock monitoring so that when writers do block other writers (or when you are not using Currently Committed semantics), you'll be able to diagnose and resolve the lock wait issue more quickly and efficiently. As with the UOW event monitor, a new LOCK event monitor can be created to enable the capture of lock timeouts, deadlocks, and lock waits for a specified duration. This monitor will show the details of the applications involved in the lock contention, including the victim and victor information, as well as detailed activity information for each of the parties involved in the locks.

Similar to the UOW event monitor, the creation of the event monitor itself does not begin to generate lock information on its own; instead, you must alter or create a workload that will begin to capture this new locking information. The `CREATE WORKLOAD` statement allows for the collection of lock timeout data, the collection of deadlock data, and the collection of lock wait data for locks waiting for more than N seconds or microseconds.

Each of the lock timeout data collectors can be collected using the `WITH HISTORY` and `WITHOUT HISTORY` options. The `WITH HISTORY` option captures and reports on all the activity for the victim and victor for each of their respective units of work. This is vital information when trying to resolve deadlocks. For example, when resolving these issues, you not only need to know who was involved in the deadlock, but what occurred during their units of work that led up to the deadlock occurring in the first place.

If you are not using DB2 WLM, you can turn on the collection of data with the following database parameters: `MON_LOCKTIMEOUT`, `MON_DEADLOCK`, and `MON_LOCKWAIT` (with its associated wait time parameter `MON_LW_THRESH`). To view the data from the new lock event monitor, you use the same interfaces described previously for UOW monitor to extract the data from the UE tables.

3
The Even More Predictable DB2: DB2 Workload Manager

Our databases are getting more powerful every day. Just a few short years ago, we would never have different applications with varying workload characteristics simultaneously accessing the same database. Today's enterprise database warehouses (EDWs) and operational data stores (ODSs) have made this a common practice. One of the consequences of this is that a robust workload management tool, acting as a doorman, resource manager, score keeper, and traffic cop all in one, has become essential to "keeping the peace" in the database system and ensuring that it's running at full throttle. Regardless of how much hardware is thrown at a database, ultimately the core CPU, memory, and I/O resources are finite by nature and should be allocated in the most appropriate and effective manner that reflects the overall priorities of the business it is supporting.

The DB2 Workload Manager (WLM) is built right into the database manager and offers a DB2 server (referred to as DB2 in this chapter) unprecedented granular control of all work running inside it. WLM was first introduced in DB2 9.5 and has been very well received: the WLM technology is powerful, comprehensive, lightweight, and granular, and it makes it easy for you to monitor DB2. In fact, if you're running DB2 9.5 and never even knew about WLM, you might be surprised to find out that it's already on and working. WLM is built into the core DB2 engine and is always "on." However, in the default setup, all the work is run at the same priority. When you license the Performance Optimization Feature Pack, you're able to configure WLM to match your business priorities and get the most you can out of your system. If you've not yet tried out WLM, the new features in DB2 9.7 make it even more compelling.

DB2 Workload Manager Basics

DB2 Workload Manager comprises four critical building blocks: service classes, workloads, thresholds, and work actions sets.

DB2 service classes serve as the primary point of resource control for all work executing in a database. All work in the database operates in a specific service class (at a granular level, we call this work an *activity*), within a two-tier hierarchy: the "parent" service *superclasses* and their children, the service *subclasses*. This hierarchy provides an easy way to share common attributes across subclasses. All work in DB2 is only executed inside a service subclass; whenever a superclass is created, a default subclass is automatically created too. All work that is sent directly to a superclass will be automatically mapped and run in its default subclass unless more action it taken (more on that in a bit).

A *DB2 workload* serves as the primary method of control for submitted work into the database. Its purpose is very clear: Workloads allow you to identify and isolate incoming database requests (connections) based on "who" submitted the request. The DB2 workload then maps these requests to a specific service class in which they will execute. This mapping occurs via connection attributes (such as an application name, an IP address, and more). Once you have customized the service classes and workloads, you can begin to map the business priorities to the database resources. You do this by differentiating between the priorities of each service class through resource allotments. In DB2 9.5, resources could be prioritized explicitly in a service class by declaring agent priority (CPU priority) and/or prefetcher priority (physical I/O priority). By assigning varying levels of these resources to different service classes, you can make certain more important work takes priority over less important work on the system. A workload executing with higher CPU and prefetcher priority will naturally execute faster than the same workload executing with lower priority levels.

DB2 thresholds are then layered on top of your database, services classes, and workloads and let you implement limits or control behaviors of database

The Even More Predictable DB2: DB2 Workload Manager

activities based on various criteria important to your business—for example, to comply with a service level agreement (SLA). Are certain applications taking up too many resources? Does the database have too many connections already? Does a query seem too expensive to run during the main part of the workday? All of these elements, both predictive and reactive, can be controlled via predefined business rules, and WLM lets you define subsequent consequences if these thresholds are breached.

Figure 3-1 shows a simple example of enabling all the basic WLM elements.

When setting up a WLM environment, you first define your service classes and then the workloads that map to them. The following example uses the client application name as the connection attribute:

```
CREATE SERVICE CLASS Marketing;
CREATE SERVICE CLASS Managers UNDER Marketing;
CREATE WORKLOAD Reporting CURRENT CLIENT_APPLNAME
  ('reporting_app') SERVICE CLASS Marketing;
CREATE WORKLOAD Summary CURRENT CLIENT_APPLNAME
  ('analytical_app') SERVICE CLASS Managers UNDER
  Marketing;
```

Once applications find their way to their runtime environment, you typically define thresholds. In the next example, one activity threshold ensures that no query that's deemed too costly is ever run (th_too_extensive).

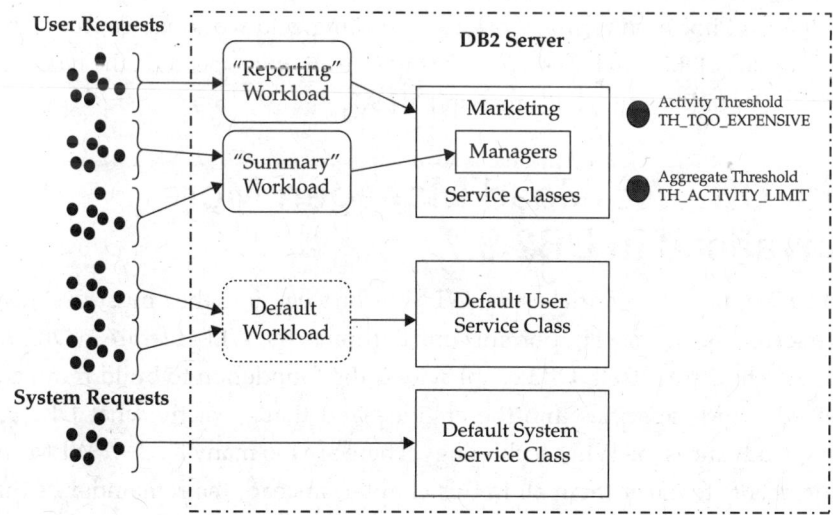

Figure 3.1 *DB2 WLM service classes, workloads, and thresholds*

In addition one aggregate threshold ensures that no more than 20 activities are ever running at any one time for this service class (th_activity_limit):

```
CREATE THRESHOLD th_too_expensive FOR SERVICE CLASS
 Marketing ACTIVITIES ENFORCEMENT DATABASE WHEN
 ESTIMATEDSQLCOST > 10000 STOP EXECUTION;
CREATE THRESHOLD th_activity_limit FOR SERVICE CLASS
 Marketing ACTIVITIES ENFORCEMENT DATABASE WHEN
 CONCURRENTDBCOORDACTIVITIES > 20 STOP EXECUTION;
```

That's all there is to setting up a basic WLM environment. To these core workload management building blocks you can add *DB2 work action sets*. These let you discriminate between different types of database activities—reads, writes, calls, Data Manipulation Language (DML), data definition language (DDL), and loads—occurring inside the database. For example, using a work action set, you could specify that only a single LOAD operation is ever running inside the database at any one time.

DB2 9.5's WLM features also introduced some powerful monitoring and control capabilities that provide real-time as well as historical monitoring capabilities. Together, they facilitate different types of monitoring—both the *push* and *pull* variety—at granular levels that allow you to retrieve the exact type of information you need, when you need it. The WLM monitoring is exposed through a number of SQL table functions, DB2 event monitors, some new SQL stored procedures, and the db2pd utility. Together, these interfaces facilitate ad hoc monitoring, workload profiling, and workload capture support for your DB2 databases. Now that you're all up to speed on the basics of WLM, let's talk about what's new in DB2 9.7.

The DB2 Workload Manager: More Advanced in DB2 9.7

DB2 9.7 significantly enriches the WLM technology into the "must-use" feature set arena. The most important contribution to the WLM feature in DB2 9.7 is the architecture itself. DB2 9.5 provided the foundation to build more advanced WLM capacities into the engine—and that's exactly what DB2 9.7 does: it advances the WLM technology. There are too many DB2 9.7 WLM enhancements to cover them all in this chapter; instead, the remainder of this chapter focuses on the main highlights and the benefits they enable.

You can group the main DB2 9.7 WLM benefits into three categories: enhanced granular control, support for priority aging (time-based tiered WLM), and faster time to value.

Enhanced Granular Control: Workload Enhancements

In WLM, incoming work is mapped to a workload via a set of connection attributes that are defined at workload creation time and are based on uniquely identifying one or more attributes of the incoming connection. DB2 9.7 introduces two small but useful enhancements to workloads: a new connection attribute and the ability to use wildcards in many of the attribute definitions.

In addition to the nine connection attributes from the previous version, DB2 9.7 introduces the new ADDRESS connection attribute that allows you to map work coming from a specific IP address (or domain name) to a specific workload. You can specify the address as either a secure domain name (that can be resolved) or an IP address in either IPv4 or IPv6 format. For example, if you wanted all work from the computer marketing01.ibm.com with IP address 9.26.27.27 to be run in the MARKETING workload, you could create this workload using either of the following statements:

```
CREATE WORKLOAD marketing ADDRESS
  ('marketing01.ibm.com');
CREATE WORKLOAD marketing ADDRESS ('9.26.27.27');
```

As previously mentioned, DB2 9.7 lets you use wildcards for application- and client-based attribute names. For example, if you had a set of user IDs numbered db2user01 to db2user05 as part of your application, you could just enter the following short statement to map them to a workload: CREATE WORKLOAD sales CURRENT CLIENT_USERID ('db2user*').

Enhanced Granular Control: Threshold Enhancements

In addition to the ten thresholds introduced in DB2 9.5, DB2 9.7 introduces five new thresholds: four activity-based thresholds (those that work on a single activity) and one aggregate-based threshold (concurrency thresholds work across multiple activities).

New Activity-based Thresholds

The four new DB2 9.7 activity level WLM thresholds are mainly used to support the new time-based tiering (more on that in a bit).

SQLROWSREAD controls the maximum number of rows that can be read on any database partition by an activity. You could use this threshold to detect and control activities that are reading an excessive number of rows. It comes with a "sister" threshold, SQLROWSREADINSC, which works the exact same way but is limited to a specific activity *per* service class as opposed to looking across the whole database.

The CPUTIME threshold can help control the maximum amount of time that an activity may consume. You'd use this threshold to detect and control activities that are consuming excessive processor resources. This threshold calculates time using a combination of both user and system processor time, which is very distinct from the ACTIVITYTOTALTIME threshold that measures the real clock time of the total activity (including the time in queue, system, and I/O wait times); CPUTIME measures only the actual CPU time used by the activity. Its sister threshold, CPUTIMEINSC, works at the activity-per-service-class level, which is also useful for priority aging.

Assume, for example, that you wanted to terminate any query on a database partition that uses more then 20 seconds of CPU time, and you want this rule checked every 5 seconds. To implement this business rule, you could create the following threshold:

```
CREATE THRESHOLD th_dbmax_cpu FOR DATABASE ACTIVITIES
  ENFORCEMENT DATABASE PARTITION WHEN CPUTIME > 20
  SECONDS CHECKING EVERY 5 SECONDS STOP EXECUTION;
```

Finally, it's worth noting that two new monitoring high watermarks have also been added to make it easier for you to determine what high values you should use with these two new thresholds:

- **act_cpu_time_top** The high watermark for processor time used by activities at all nesting levels in a workload, service class, or work class
- **act_rows_read_top** The high watermark for the number of rows read by activities at all nesting levels in a workload, service class, or work class

The New Aggregate-based Threshold

DB2 9.7 also introduces a new aggregate threshold, AGGSQLTEMPSPACE, that controls the maximum amount of system temporary table space that can be consumed in total across all activities in a service class (on a single database partition). You would use this threshold to detect and control activities that belong to a service class whose activities are consuming too much system temporary table space. For example, if you wanted to be alerted when the temporary space consumed by the Marketing department was greater then a 100MB, you could create the following threshold:

```
CREATE THRESHOLD th_detect_high_tmps FOR SERVICE CLASS
SYSDEFAULTSUBCLASS UNDER "Marketing" ACTIVITIES
ENFORCEMENT DATABASE PARTITION WHEN AGGSQLTEMPSPACE >
100 M COLLECT ACTIVITY DATA CONTINUE;
```

Notice that this threshold works at the service subclass level, and in this case on the SYSDEFAULTSUBCLASS subclass (the default subclass for the Marketing service class).

Thresholds at Workload Level

Applications are differentiated from each other via workloads, which is always good even if you're not planning to place them in different service classes. Workloads take up almost no resources and increase granular control of what is running on the system. In DB2 9.5, thresholds were generally defined at the database or service class level, and this could have limited your ability to specify rules that target specific workloads unless they also target specific service classes too. DB2 9.7 makes this process easier by allowing you to define thresholds *at the workload level* for many important thresholds. This avoids having to isolate applications from each other in separate service classes if that isn't your preference; instead, you can keep these applications in the same service class and differentiate them based on workload attributes. Specifically, DB2 9.7 now enables the already existing ESTIMATEDSQLCOST, SQLROWSRETURNED, ACTIVITYTOTALTIME, and SQLTEMPSPACE thresholds to be defined at the workload level, and it adds the two new workload-defined thresholds, SQLROWSREAD and CPUTIME, discussed earlier.

Enhanced Granular Control: Service Class Enhancements

As mentioned, in DB2 9.5 resources can be prioritized between service classes by CPU or prefetch I/O priority. CPU priority can be allocated via the setting of the DB2 agent priority level or via the OS system WLM infrastructure. The former affects the relative priority to other agent threads running on the database server, while the latter provides granular control right to the CPU time slice. Prefetcher I/O priority is allocated via assigning a priority to the DB2 prefetch requests—directly influencing the order in which such requests are processed by DB2. All higher priority prefetcher requests are processed before any lower level requests even start.

DB2 9.7 adds yet another powerful resource control: controlling logical I/O via *buffer pool priority*. This new control allows you to assign buffer pool priority to a service class (HIGH, MEDIUM, or LOW), which directly impacts the page victim algorithm that determines whether a data page fetched by activities in a service class is a candidate to be swapped out of memory (if memory is needed). This means work running in a service class with a higher priority will usually have its pages live longer inside the buffer pool versus lower priority pages, and hence its activities should run with an improved throughput if memory is limited.

What systems are most likely to benefit from this new resource differentiator? Those with the highest current buffer pool contention between applications. You can measure this simply by looking at the overall hit ratio of your buffer pools: how many times does DB2 find a page it needs in the buffer pool as opposed to having to fetch it from disk. We recommend that you consider using this new resource control for those applications with a less than or equal to 85 percent buffer cache hit ratio (meaning 15 percent of the time or more required data pages aren't in the buffer pool). You can set the buffer pool priority in DB2 9.7 to DEFAULT, LOW, MEDIUM, or HIGH. As you would expect, service subclasses inherit their priority from their service superclass, and this control is no different.

WLM Goes Linux

A key strategy for DB2 WLM is to have it integrate nicely with the most popular external WLM infrastructures used in today's enterprises. As a first step in this direction, DB2 9.5 shipped with tight integration into an AIX WLM environment. DB2 9.7 extends the reach of a holistic workload management look by

The Even More Predictable DB2: DB2 Workload Manager

offering the same tight integration level with the Linux operating system (you need to be running a Linux kernel at the 2.6.26 version or later). As of DB2 9.7, whether you're running Linux or AIX, you can supercharge your control of CPU resources for your DB2 service classes by allocating CPU shares that can be adjusted dynamically, "borrow" unused CPU shares from other service classes, and benefit from deeper OS-level statistics for your service classes.

To use your Linux WLM alongside the DB2 WLM, you first create your Linux service classes, then map all your DB2 service classes (including the default ones) to these Linux classes, and then manage the entire environment from the OS level. We recommend you use a 1:1 mapping between DB2 service classes and Linux classes; this allows you to adjust the Linux processor shares easily in each DB2 service class individually, as shown in Figure 3-2.

If you wanted to map the DB2 service classes to the Linux WLM service classes shown in Figure 3-2, you would alter the service class and use the OUTBOUND CORRELATOR keyword as follows:

```
ALTER SERVICE CLASS Marketing OUTBOUND CORRELATOR
'_DB2_Marketing';
ALTER SERVICE CLASS Managers UNDER Marketing OUTBOUND
CORRELATOR '_DB2_Managers';
ALTER SERVICE CLASS SYSDEFAULTUSERCLASS OUTBOUND
CORRELATOR '_DB2_DEF_USER';
ALTER SERVICE CLASS SYSDEFAULTSYSTEMCLASS OUTBOUND
CORRELATOR '_DB2_DEF_SYS';
```

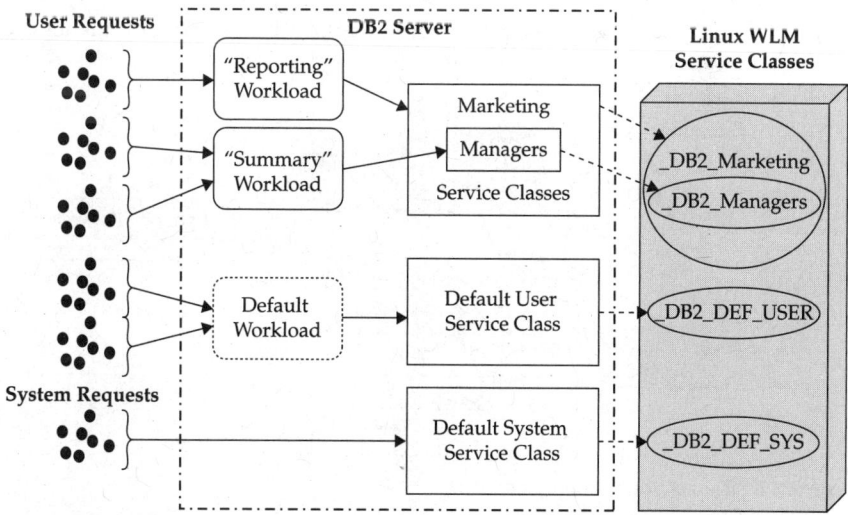

Figure 3.2 *Integration of DB2 WLM with Linux WLM*

Priority Aging Workload Management

Are you tired of longer queries hogging all the resources on your system at the expense of the shorter, but more important, tactical queries? One of the major new features of DB2 9.7 is support for a new type of workload management approach called *priority aging*.

Priority aging automatically decreases the priority of longer running activities such that the throughput for shorter running activities can be improved. In DB2 9.7, WLM can make changes to the priority of in-progress activities by moving them (we call this *remapping*) between service classes in response to a certain threshold being violated: specifically in DB2 9.7, the amount of processor time used or the number of rows read. This will automatically decrease, or age, the priority of longer running activities. And because DB2 performs the remapping automatically, it's simple, consistent, and doesn't require any detailed knowledge of the current activities running on your database.

Figure 3-3 shows an example of priority aging. As work enters the system, activities are automatically placed into the first service subclass and begin running using its high-priority settings. After the violation of a certain threshold (5 seconds of CPU time in this example), DB2 dynamically reassigns the running activity to the next lower service class. This dynamic resource control is repeatedly applied until the activity completes or ends up in the lowest priority class, where it remains until it is completes.

Before DB2 9.7, three actions could be performed when a threshold was violated: STOP EXECUTION, which automatically stops the running activity

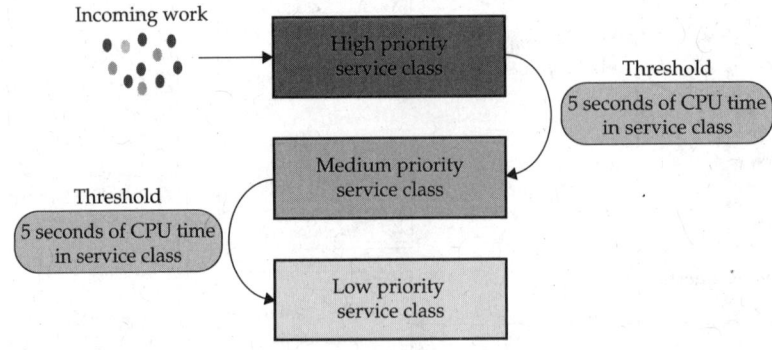

Figure 3.3 *Tiered priority aging concept*

when the threshold is violated and returns an error code to the submitting application; CONTINUE, which permits the activity to run but collects relevant data in a threshold violation event monitor for DBAs to perform future analysis; and COLLECT ACTITIVTY DATA, which is used with either CONTINUE or STOP to allow you to capture more detailed information about the activity that violated the threshold.

You implement tiered priority aging using the new REMAP ACTIVITY threshold violation action—added in DB2 9.7 to the existing ones detailed in the preceding paragraph. If a threshold is violated with this setting, DB2 lets the activity continue but automatically remaps the running workload to a new service class. Of course, the net effect depends on how you set up the service classes: the priority of the activity increases if the new service class has more resources, and it decreases if it has fewer resources. You can think of this class as a special case of CONTINUE; in both cases, there is no explicit indication to the end user or application that a threshold was violated (just the implicit performance impact of running in the new service class).

Our Tiered Priority Aging Recommendations

Our testing has shown that a simple three-tiered approach can help increase the throughput for short queries on a heavily loaded system. To get started in this area, we recommend that you create a series of service classes with successively lower levels of resource priorities (HIGH, MEDIUM, and LOW). Next, create a few threshold actions that move activities between these service subclasses in order, from HIGH to LOW, based on time spent or rows read metrics.

In DB2 9.7, you can use one of the two new "INSC" activity thresholds, detailed earlier, to trigger the movement of running activities between service classes: processor time used (CPUTIMEINSC) and the number of rows read by an application (SQLROWSREADINSC). On databases where the primary resource activities have to compete for processor time, we recommend you use the CPUTIMEINSC threshold as your first measure of control. On databases where queries reading many table rows result primarily in I/O contention, we recommend you use the SQLROWSREADINSC threshold. Finally, on systems that see a combination of heavy processor and I/O activity, we recommend you consider both thresholds.

A Tiered Priority Aging Example: Buying Should Always Be Fast!

Assume that you're in charge of a Web site that sells books. Furthermore, the business has asked your IT department to ensure that you optimize the experience for clients buying and performing cart activities on the Web site. With this in mind, you want to make sure that shorter shopping basket transactions, usually consisting of cart-related activities such as adding a book or a purchasing operation, are always given the highest priority, even if the system is swamped with longer transactions (such as searching and sorting books, which is indicative of browsing type queries and broad user searches performed by the general public). To accommodate this preferential treatment, you can leverage the tiered priority aging feature in DB2 9.7 to assist your in implementing this business policy.

Start by creating the service classes and the workload. Set up three tiers named after their expected query length: SHORT, MEDIUM, and LONG. Each will be differentiated to the maximum extent using all three resource controls we've introduced in DB2 9.7. This example will also use the new connection attribute wildcard feature, since in this example all client application names start with the phrase db2books:

```
CREATE SERVICE CLASS WLM_BOOKS_APP;
CREATE SERVICE CLASS WLM_SHORT UNDER WLM_BOOKS_APP
AGENT PRIORITY -20 PREFETCH
 PRIORITY HIGH BUFFERPOOL PRIORITY HIGH;
CREATE SERVICE CLASS WLM_MEDIUM UNDER WLM_BOOKS_APP
AGENT PRIORITY 0 PREFETCH
 PRIORITY MEDIUM BUFFERPOOL PRIORITY MEDIUM;
CREATE SERVICE CLASS WLM_LONG UNDER WLM_BOOKS_APP AGENT
PRIORITY 20 PREFETCH PRIORITY
 LOW BUFFERPOOL PRIORITY LOW;
CREATE WORKLOAD db2_books CURRENT
CLIENT_APPLNAME('db2books*') SERVICE CLASS
 WLM_BOOKS_APP;
```

> **NOTE:** *Agent priority values used in this example are for UNIX or Linux operating systems, which uses a –20 to +20 scale. On Windows, the scale is from +6 to –6 and is reversed. So in this example we would replace –20 with +6 and +20 with –6 on a Windows-based DB2 server.*

Notice that this example maps all the work to the service superclass WLM_BOOKS_APP. To ensure that the most important work (DML and CALL statements) starts in the WLM_SHORT service subclass, you will need to define a work action set to grab this type of activity and map it appropriately. Here's an example:

```
CREATE WORK CLASS SET WLM_TIERS_WCS
  (WORK CLASS dml_wc WORK TYPE DML, WORK CLASS call_wc
WORK TYPE CALL,
   WORK CLASS other_wc WORK TYPE ALL);
CREATE WORK ACTION SET wlm_tiers_was FOR SERVICE CLASS
WLM_BOOKS_APP USING WORK CLASS
  SET WLM_TIERS_WCS
  (WORK ACTION dml_wa ON WORK CLASS dml_wc MAP ACTIVITY
TO WLM_SHORT,
   WORK ACTION call_wa ON WORK CLASS call_wc MAP
ACTIVITY TO WLM_SHORT,
   WORK ACTION other_wc ON WORK CLASS other_wc MAP
ACTIVITY TO WLM_
MEDIUM);
```

The preceding DDL also instructs DB2 to map all other *recognized* non-DML and non-CALL activities to the WLM_MEDIUM tier. Note that all non-recognized activities that are not SQL or LOAD-based (such as BACKUP, RESTORE, and REORG utilities) will be run in the default subclass.

Finally, to implement this example, you need to create thresholds that will perform the automatic remapping between the defined service subclasses. The following DDL ages activity after 2 seconds of CPU time are consumed and then again after an additional 4 seconds of CPU time are consumed:

```
CREATE THRESHOLD wlm_tiers_remap_short_to_medium FOR
SERVICE CLASS WLM_SHORT UNDER
  WLM_BOOKS_APP ACTIVITIES ENFORCEMENT DATABASE
PARTITION WHEN CPUTIMEINSC > 2 SECONDS
  CHECKING EVERY 1 SECONDS REMAP ACTIVITY TO WLM_MEDIUM;
CREATE THRESHOLD wlm_tiers_remap_medium_to_long FOR
SERVICE CLASS WLM_MEDIUM UNDER
  WLM_BOOKS_APP ACTIVITIES ENFORCEMENT DATABASE
PARTITION WHEN CPUTIMEINSC > 4 SECONDS
  CHECKING EVERY 1 SECONDS REMAP ACTIVITY TO WLM_LONG;
```

Flattening the Time to Value Curve for DB2 WLM Technology

Some clients have a good grasp of the workloads running in their environment and can express their relative priority to their businesses. For these clients, setting up WLM is a relativity simple planning and scripting exercise.

However, not all clients that we talk to are so fortunate. In fact, lots of IT shops don't have a good grasp of what's actually running on their databases. If you mix this with the unfamiliarity associated with a new feature such as WLM, you may need a helping hand to get started. This section is all about the "little in effort but big impact" thoughtful things the WLM development team did to help you gain control of your database runtimes and leverage the rich capabilities of WLM in no time at all.

Sample Scripts

To help clients quickly and easily roll out their own priority aging WLM environment, DB2 9.7 ships with two sample setup scripts (you can find them in the `samples/admin_scripts` directory). These scripts create service classes, workloads, and thresholds to implement priority aging and a simple three-tiered configuration very similar to the example in the preceding section. In the provided sample scripts, the focus of workload management is around maximizing the overall throughput of the system. Quite simply, these scripts create an environment in which every query has a fair opportunity to finish its work quickly, and if it does not, then it gradually starts decreasing in priority and the resources that are available for it to consume.

Both scripts create a WLM hierarchy that gives shorter activities more priority, and both use the `CPUTIMEINSC` threshold to remap activities. The scripts differ, however, on how activities are first mapped to a service class: the first script does initial mapping based on *activity type*, while the second does it based on *estimated cost*. Refer to the DB2 documentation for more information.

New Web-based WLM Tooling

Before DB2 9.7, you could graphically configure a WLM environment using the Design Studio that ships with InfoSphere Warehouse. In DB2 9.7, a much improved web-based graphical tool (shown in Figure 3-4) replaces the previous generation WLM tooling that drastically cuts the time to implement a new WLM environment. As of DB2 9.7, the new InfoSphere Warehouse Workload Manager helps you set up and configure WLM and make changes to your workloads or priorities. This new tool provides a simple yet powerful tool whose sole purpose is to help a DBA get up and running with WLM as quickly as possible. The new toolset helps with the understanding and definition of workloads running on your system—for most of us, the most challenging

The Even More Predictable DB2: DB2 Workload Manager

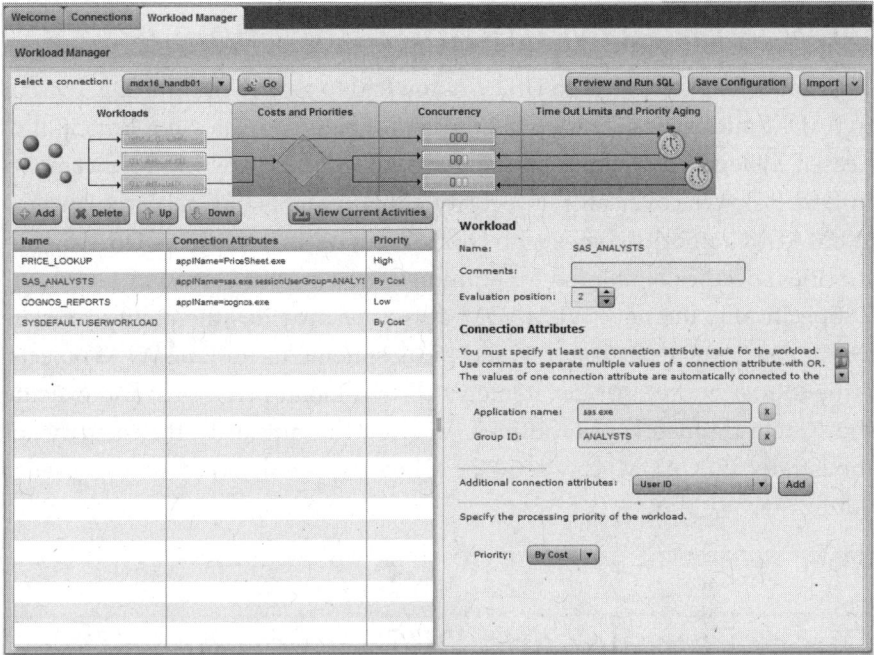

Figure 3.4 *InfoSphere Warehouse 9.7 Workload Manager Web tool makes it a lot easier to configure a workload management environment.*

part—as well as hiding the seldom used details; bottom line, we like the new WLM tooling because it allows you to learn as you go but not get overwhelmed. The new Workload Manager toolset even has some WLM best practices built right in!

Figure 3-4 shows the main screen from this new WLM tool. This tool will automatically create a single service super class and then assist you in creating your own custom workloads, including viewing current activities in the database. Furthermore, it allows you to specify priorities for different categories of work and to separate activities according to their priority and cost to your business.

From an operational perspective, the Optim Performance Manager (formerly known as the DB2 Performance Expert) provides extensive monitoring and historical analysis capabilities and offers a number of tightly integrated reporting elements in WLM. You can use this tool to monitor and analyze how your system is performing, both in real time and historically.

New WLMADM Authorization Role

To administer WLM prior to DB2 9.7, you had to grant a user the DBADM or SYSADM authorities. This over-granting of rights violates the Principal of Lease Privilege. You'll find a lot of least privilege security work enhancements in DB2 9.7. (We cover all the security enhancements in Chapter 4.) A new WLMADM authority comes with DB2 9.7, which has a subset of DBADM authorities specifically tailored for administration of WLM objects.

Specifically, the new WLMADM authority provides the ability to issue CREATE, ALTER, COMMENT ON, and DROP statements for DB2 WLM objects; issue GRANT and REVOKE statements for workload privileges; and execute the system-defined WLM routines. To grant this authority, the security administrator (SECADM) can issue the following command to allow a user to administer WLM:

GRANT WLMADM ON DATABASE TO USER <user_name>;

Query Patroller and DB2 Governor Now Deprecated

Although not officially deprecated with the release of DB2 9.5, the writing has been on the wall for these previous generation tools. In consideration of the enhanced tooling, priority aging support, new thresholds, and workload enhancements, DB2 Query Patroller (DB2 QP) and DB2 Governor have now been officially deprecated. They will no longer be enhanced in any way and will be a candidate for removal from the product portfolio in a future release.

It's easy to get to WLM from a DB2 QP environment since WLM is designed to run concurrently with DB2 QP workloads by default; this gives you an opportunity to move workloads into WLM objects slowly over time. Specifically, any work submitted in the default user service class for execution in a DB2 QP environment is intercepted and sent to DB2 QP. Work submitted for execution in other service classes defined by the DBA will bypass DB2 QP completely. Look for a migration script (likely to be packaged as part of a Fix Pack) that allows you to make the transition even easier.

4

The Even More Secure DB2: The DB2 Security Blanket

Data is the lifeblood of an enterprise. It shouldn't be surprising to anyone that as data becomes more central to running our businesses, protecting the data becomes more critical as well. Unfortunately, even with the growing focus on data security in recent years, studies tell us that companies aren't doing a good enough job of protecting data. According to privacyrights.org, more than 260 million data records were lost or stolen since 2005 in the United States alone! This overall trend is generally getting worse, with 2008 going down as another record-breaking year for data loss.

In the "old" days, we could shrug it off as problem for the government sector or financial industry. No more, however; in fact, the five largest US data breaches of 2008 occurred in five different industries: banking, retail, healthcare, insurance, and government. No matter what your industry, properly securing data has become an imperative.

Driven by these stark numbers, and the high profile data breaches that have made their way to the front pages of blogs, magazines, and newspapers alike, those tasked with managing databases are on the front lines of data protection. DBAs are bombarded with orders to ensure that data is secure, as well as requests to comply with an ever-increasing number of regulations; whether it's Sarbanes-Oxley (SOX), Payment Card Industry Data Security Standard (PCI DSS), Health Insurance Portability and Accountability Act (HIPPA), the Basel Accord's Basel II, or some other governing regulation, the bottom line is that you need to comply and the CIO, CSO, and even the CEO are all watching you!

The DB2 server (referred to as DB2 in this chapter) is rightfully regarded as one of the most secure databases on the market, a reputation derived from an effective security model, a focus on secure development, its basket of advanced security features, and its long history of successfully securing a good deal of the world's data. This leadership continues with the DB2 9.7. For example, DB2 9.7 has already achieved the internationally recognized Common Criteria certification used by governments and other organizations to assess the security and assurance of technology products.

DB2 9.7 includes many new security-related enhancements. If we look at the key highlights, we can group them into two categories: authorization-related security enhancements and data-in-motion encryption enhancements.

In this chapter, we'll delve into the new features that help you implement tighter and more rigorous security controls in your IT shops. From a broadening of the "principal of least privilege," to a new hierarchy of privileges and authorities, to the more granular separation of duties, to Secure Sockets Layer (SSL) encryption for data-in-motion protection, DB2 9.7 offers lots of goodies to protect your sensitive data and meet the ever-demanding governance requirements placed on your data.

The IBM Data Server Security Blueprint

DB2 has long since provided a myriad of security capabilities to help ensure that your data is locked down and secure; the DB2 9.7 release goes even further. That said, technological capabilities in and of themselves are only half the picture; they must be supported by sensible security policies and best practices. With this in mind, before we dive into the details about the new security features of DB2 9.7 and how they will assist your compliance efforts (and, trust us, they will), let's take a moment to look at an indispensible document released last year that can help simplify your overall data security planning efforts around DB2.

One of the major challenges in data security is getting database personnel, who are for the most part not security people, to understand the serious threats to their databases and then choosing the best countermeasures to mitigate or eliminate these threats from the many available options. Vendors tend to spend a lot of ink describing how security features work, but unfortunately not enough attention is paid to explaining what exact threats a particular security feature was built to deal with and when it should best be used versus a different option. For example, does using data encryption mean that you no longer need to use Label-Based Access Control (LBAC) techniques to protect your tables? What is the best approach to protect your databases from internal threats? When do you use data masking and what does it protect against? How do the various layers of security all fit together? These types of questions are asked every day, and clear, consistent answers are required; we're going to tell you about a place you can get them (you can thank us later): the *IBM Data Server Security Blueprint*.

These sample questions were actually the driving motivation that led to the creation of the IBM Data Server Security Blueprint. IBM convened a group of IBM data security experts, including thought leaders in security, to devise a blueprint to help customers understand the most important threats that they are up against, and to recommend the best current countermeasures to these threats. This resulted in the creation of the IBM Data Server Security Blueprint and the subsequent DB2 Best Practice for Security (the latter is based fully on the former). The purpose of these threat-centric documents is to assist customers in data security planning to protect data inside IBM databases. (Notice we used "databases" here, because this document is as applicable to DB2 running on Windows as it is to DB2 running on z/OS, and even Informix.)

Organized in a short, easy-to-understand format, the blueprint is essentially a single page diagram that communicates its content in a simple, consistent, three-column format: threats, countermeasures, and the features needed to implement the countermeasures. A companion whitepaper details the security blueprint, the selected threats and countermeasures proposed by the blueprint, and more. The overall layered architecture of the Data Server Security Blueprint is depicted in Figure 4-1.

We strongly recommend that you read this document before building a data security policy for your environment. By reading this document, you'll get a strong foundation for understanding data security, the threat landscape, and how to architect effective countermeasures that leverage the power of DB2. The IBM Data Server Security Blueprint can be downloaded at www.ibm.com/software/data/db2imstools/solutions/security-blueprint.html. In addition, you can get the DB2 Security Best Practices white paper at http://download.boulder.ibm.com/ibmdl/pub/software/dw/dm/db2/bestpractices/DB2BP_Security_0508I.pdf.

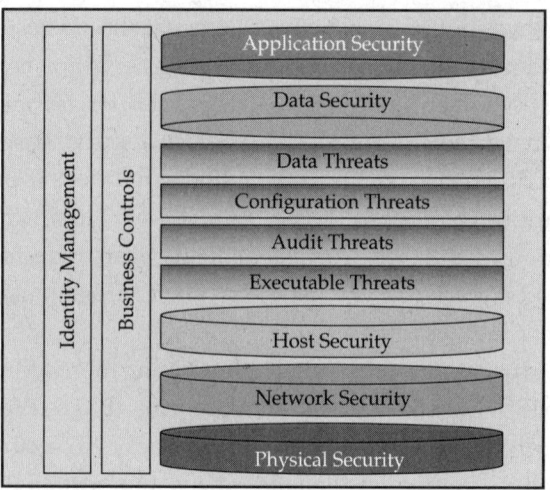

Figure 4.1 The IBM Data Server Security Blueprint architecture: your path to data protection

Authorization-Related Security Enhancements

Access control is the foundation of database security, and authorization in turn is the foundation of access control. Authorization ensures that only those with the right to access a piece of data are able to access it, and no one else. Two fundamental security principles have been proven, time and time again over decades, to be invaluable for effective data security: *separation of duties* and the *principle of least privilege*. Because of the large security benefits derived from these principles, you will find them as requirements in some form or another in almost *all* the important security or privacy regulations today.

As one of the most fundamental data security principles, the principle of separation of duties states that to prevent fraud and decrease the chance of human error, you should spread out the privileges needed for an important function or process among two or more people without overlap. A single user should never possess unlimited authority; instead, privileges are assigned in a manner such that no one person can control a process from start to finish. When more than one person is involved in a process, the probability of fraud occurring is greatly decreased; only when multiple parties collude to commit fraud would it be successfully perpetrated. A common example of this principle is a safely deposit box at a bank: both the box's owner and a bank employee must insert their keys to open the safely deposit box.

The principle of least privilege (also referred to as the principle of least authority) states that a user should be granted only the minimum privileges required to fulfill their assigned work, and nothing more. This approach decreases the surface area of the security risk that the user entails to the minimum possible, whether that risk stems from malicious intent, the user's ID being compromised, or most commonly a negligent mistake. For example, if a person is responsible for database maintenance, such as performing backup and recovery operations, she should be given only these privileges and nothing more. Such employees should not be able to view or modify data directly in the database, and they definitely should not be able to grant this ability to anyone else, since these privileges aren't required for them to be able to do their assigned job of backing up and restoring the database.

So what do these two security principles have to do with DB2 9.7? Well, the overriding objective of the many authorization-related security enhancements in DB2 9.7 is to make it easy to implement these critical security principles. In this section, we'll look at both of them in detail.

Separation of Duties between Database and Security Administration

The most important place to implement separation of duties in DB2, or any database system for that matter, is between the DBA who owns the administration of the database and the security administrator who's responsible for the security of the database. The separation between administration and security functions greatly decreases the risk of an internal threat and can greatly enhance data security in your environment. For the same reason, the separation of duties is a key requirement for security-related regulations.

DB2 has been gradually heading toward more separation of duties for a couple of versions now; starting with the introduction of the DB2 Security Administrator (SECADM) authority in DB2 9, and the gradual reduction of the security-related capabilities of the System Administrator (SYSADM) and Database Administrator (DBADM) authorities. As you may recall, in DB2, the instance-level SYSADM authority is the highest system-level authority, the database-level DBADM authority is highest database-level authority, and the SECADM authority is the highest security-related authority. In DB2 9.7, this separation of duties has been fully reached between these key roles: you can now easily administer a DB2 database, out of the box, with full separation of the duties between the SYSADM, the DBADM, and the SECADM. The SYSADM and DBADM focus on administering the system and the database, respectively, while the SECADM focuses on managing the security and authorizations of the database.

So what specifically has changed to make this full separation possible in DB2 9.7? First, DB2 has centralized the ability to access data (read, write, or modify) and the ability to grant privileges or authorities at the database level to two new authorities: DATAACCESS and ACCESSCTRL. The new DATAACCESS authority provides the user with all the privileges needed to access data inside a specific database: SELECT, UPDATE, INSERT, DELETE, and LOAD privileges on all tables, views, Materialized Query Tables (MQTs), and nicknames in the database, as well EXECUTE privileges on all packages and routines. The new ACCESSCTRL authority provides a user with most of the privileges needed to manage access control on the database—namely, all those the DBADM used to be able to do automatically in the last version of DB2: GRANT and REVOKE all object privileges, and GRANT many database authorities. Note that we said most, and not all, of the access control privileges. Some capabilities are still the sole domain of the SECADM authority and are *not* provided to those with ACCESSCTRL authority. Specifically these are GRANT and REVOKE of the key database authorities: SECADM, DBADM, DATAACCESS and ACCESSCTRL, GRANT and REVOKE of database roles, GRANT and REVOKE of the WITH ADMIN option, and GRANT and REVOKE of security labels and exemptions for LBAC.

As you probably guessed, SECADM receives and always possesses the ACCESSCTRL authority; SECADM is always a superset of the ACCESSCTRL authority. As for the DATAACCESS authority, a lot has changed. Before DB2 9.7, a user assigned to DBADM used to get this authority by default; this changed in DB2 9.7 and falls under the sole discretion of the SECADM. As of DB2 9.7, default DATAACCESS authority is now an option of the GRANT DBADM command and is not automatically inherited in the granting of DBADM unless the SECADM wants it to be. It's important to wrap your head around this, because the rest of the authorization-related enhancements in DB2 9.7 flow from this key change and revolve around the three critical administrator authorities in DB2: SYSADM, DBADM, and SECADM.

In DB2 9.7, the SYSADM authority no longer receives implicit DBADM authority on all the databases in the instance. In fact, in DB2 9.7, SYSADM *doesn't get* the DATAACCESS authority on the database, meaning that SYSADM no longer receives the ability to read, write, or modify any data in the database, Quite simply, in DB2 9.7, possessing any instance-level authority doesn't automatically provide *any* access to data in the database. In addition, SYSADM no longer has the ability to GRANT or REVOKE any database-level authorities or object privileges; the notable exception are table space privileges, which are still under SYSADM control by default. In DB2 9.7, SYSADM can assign only instance-level authorities (remember, *without* data access). All other security management roles are now the sole domain of the SECADM.

You should be aware that even though the SYSADM no longer receives implicit DBADM authority for all databases in their instance, if the SYSADM is the creator of the database, the SYSADM *will still* receive SECADM and DBADM authorities on that database by default. This is done to support simple use cases (or embedded environments), where all three roles are performed by the same individual. In security conscious enterprise environments, where the SECADM and the DBADM roles are being filled by different individuals, these authorities can and should be removed from the SYSADM, as you will see shortly in an example.

Lastly, looking at the SECADM authority, it's clear that those possessing this authority have now become the sole owners of security in a database. New in DB2 9.7, this now includes the ability to GRANT and REVOKE DBADM authority directly. In addition, since it's so important now, the SECADM authority can now be granted to a role or group, making it much easier to vest this authority to multiple users who need it.

Here's an example to illustrate all of these changes in DB2 9.7. Assume you want to create a secure database that implements separation of duties between a company's administration staff (SYSADM and DBADM) and its security staff (SECADM). Assume that the SYSADM Eaton issued a CREATE DATABASE command and in so doing received DBADM and SECADM authority on the database. Eaton's first action would be to assign the SECADM authority to the designated security administrator (Tassi). This scenario is shown below:

```
CREATE DATABASE secure_db AUTOMATIC STORAGE YES
RESTRICTIVE;
CONNECT TO secure_db;
GRANT SECADM ON DATABASE TO USER Tassi;
```

Notice that Eaton can issue the GRANT SECADM command *not* because of his SYSADM authority, but because he currently possesses SECADM authority.

With this in mind, it stands to reason that a security administrator's first task should be to revoke the implicit SECADM and DBADM authorities from the SYSADM. Next, the SECADM should assign the DBADM to the proper administrator (in this case, Baklarz), but *without* giving him the ability to access the data in the database or to grant others privileges on the database. To implement this security policy, the SECADM Tassi would enter the following commands:

```
REVOKE SECADM, DBADM ON DATABASE FROM USER Eaton;
GRANT DBADM WITHOUT DATAACCESS WITHOUT ACCESSCTRL ON
DATABASE TO USER Baklarz;
```

After entering these commands, you now have a secure database managed with a true separation of duties between three administrators: the system administrator, the database administrator, and the security administrator. This type of security topology would surely be a great step in keeping your auditors happy and, more importantly, your environment more secure!

Principle of Least Privilege

To implement the principle of least privilege in a database, authorities have to be available for assignment in a granular fashion. In consideration of this, the main enhancements in DB2 9.7 to help implement this principle make privileges that previously necessitated DBADM authority available in a more granular fashion. In the preceding sections, we introduced two of the most important of these new database-level authorities: ACCESSCTRL and DATAACCESS, in which are vested the data access and data access control capabilities at the database level. To support the principle of least privilege, three new database-level authorities have also been introduced: EXPLAIN, SQLADM, and WLMADM.

The new EXPLAIN authority provides the privileges required to run EXPLAIN and PREPARE dynamic and static SQL statements, and DESCRIBE an output of a SELECT or XQuery statement. The new SQLADM authority, in addition to including the EXPLAIN authority, provides the ability to monitor and tune SQL in general. This includes privileges such as CREATE or DROP EVENT MONITOR, FLUSH EVENT MONITOR, FLUSH OPTIMIZATION PROFILE CACHE, FLUSH PACKAGE CACHE, REORG INDEXES or TABLE, RUNSTATS, and SET EVENT MONITOR STATE.

Although it's outside the scope of this book to discuss static SQL, we'd like to note that static SQL (which can be attained without any application change using the IBM Optim pureQuery technology) provides a synergistic approach to the principal of least privilege and furthermore helps protect you database against what some consider the world's number one vulnerability: the SQL injection attack. Finally, a user with the new WLMADM authority can manage all of the Workload Manager (WLM) constructs (see Chapter 3). This includes the privileges to execute CREATE, ALTER, COMMENT ON, and DROP statements for the following WLM manager objects: service classes, workloads, thresholds, work action sets, work class sets, and histogram templates. In addition, this authority includes the privileges to issue GRANT and REVOKE statements for workload privileges and to execute the system-defined WLM management routines.

You should be aware that all three of these new authorities are still held by DBADM, but they can also be held and delegated to others as well. You no longer need to be given the entire DBADM authority spectrum (which would grant more authorities needed to perform a job and therefore violate the principle of least privilege) to run these operations. Any security administrator or a user with ACCESSCTRL authority can assign these new authorities to users, groups, or roles using the GRANT statement.

Figure 4-2 shows the authorities available at the database level as of DB2 9.7. Note the clear separation of duties between the SECADM and the DBADM.

Another small but important change to help implement the principle of least privilege at the database level in DB2 9.7 is to make the EXECUTE privilege sufficient enough to run all three database-level audit routines: AUDIT_ARCHIVE, AUDIT_LIST_LOGS, and AUDIT_DELIM_EXTRACT.

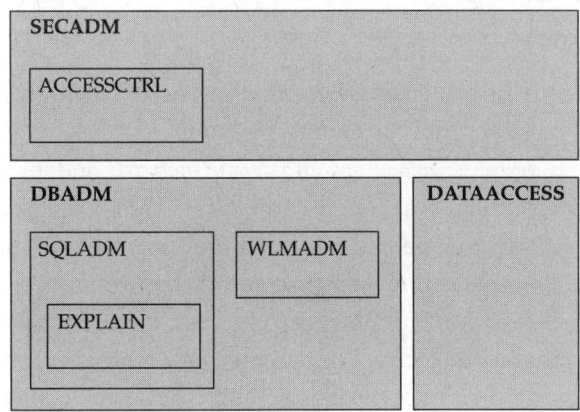

Figure 4.2 *Database-level authorities as of DB2 9.7*

In other words, you no longer need to grant someone SECADM just to be able to call these routines. Note, however, that SECADM is still the ultimate owner of what's being audited on the database: SECADM is required to create new or modify existing audit policies.

At the instance level, DB2 still has the same four instance-level authorities available with previous versions of DB2: SYSADM, SYSCTRL, SYSMAINT, and SYSMON. We've already discussed the changes to SYSADM in terms of removing many of its implicit database-level capabilities in the preceding section. The only other significant changes for instance-level authorities in DB2 9.7 are the additional privileges added to the SYSMON authority to improve database monitoring capabilities of users holding this authority. As of DB2 9.7, SYSMON now includes the ability to run additional LIST commands and run the db2mtrk command for memory pool allocation reporting.

Finally, we can't stress enough that none of the authorities in DB2 9.7, whether instance- or database-level, implicitly provide the ability to access the actual data in the database; if you want to access data, you need to have DATAACCESS authority. For example, a user who holds SQLADM authority can monitor the SQL running on the system but cannot actually run a SELECT statement and view the data in the base table (he or she would require the SELECT privilege or DATAACCESS authority to get at this data). The separation of duties and principle of least privilege ideologies work together to make your databases safer and more secure and DB2 9.7 ensures that implementing these best practices is easier than ever.

SSL Enhancements for Data-in-Motion Protection

Sensitive data must be protected wherever it is. Since it directly affects the types of threats and most appropriate countermeasures, we usually talk about protecting data in two states: *data at rest* and *data in motion*. For data at rest, we recommend implementing data encryption using IBM Database Encryption Expert (to protect against people not using the "front door") and DB2's Advanced Access Control Feature Pack (to control what "rooms they can access"). See "IBM Data Server Security Blueprint" in this chapter for more details.

For data in motion, the focus of this section, DB2 relies primarily on encryption techniques. In previous versions of DB2, this usually meant using the DATA_ENCRYPT option for client connectivity, since it was the only available option that was built into DB2 and was simple to enable. However, this option was starting to get a little "long in the tooth," primarily because it uses the older Data Encryption Standard (DES) encryption algorithm that uses a 56-bit key. To address this issue and ensure that DB2 users have a current security infrastructure for data in motion, DB2 9.7 introduces built-in support for the industry-standard SSL encryption and its successor, Transport Layer Security (TLS).

> **NOTE:** We'll refer to SSL and TLS as SSL for the remainder of this chapter to keep things simple.

In addition to using the latest secure encryption algorithm, the Advanced Encryption Standard (AES) uses 256-bit keys, DB2's SSL implementation meets all the requirements of the Federal Information Processing Standards (FIPS) 140-2 and is therefore considered *FIPS compliant*. FIPS compliance is important because it's a common requirement for government installations and some regulations call it out explicitly.

The SSL encryption is provided by the IBM Global Security Kit (GSKit), which is now automatically installed when you install DB2. The GSKit provides a fully FIPS-compliant cipher suite, which in addition to encryption, allows you to ensure data integrity through Message Authentication Codes (MAC). DB2 9.7 provides support for all DB2 clients as well as simplified SSL setup.

DB2 9.7 SSL Supports for All Clients

SSL support was first made available in DB2 9 Fix Pack 2; however, when it was released it supported only Java clients. That was a great story for those applications built on Java, but it obviously didn't help other data access methods such as .NET, command line interface (CLI), and more. As of DB2 9.7, SSL data-in-motion encryption is now fully supported for *all* DB2 client types, including those using CLI/Open Database Connectivity (ODBC), embedded SQL, .NET, and more.

Simplified SSL Setup

If you've ever tried to set up SSL encryption in DB2 9, then you know it's a pretty extensive effort and learning curve—all external to DB2. In DB2 9.7, much of this configuration has been integrated into DB2 as database manager configuration parameters and has been greatly simplified. Setup has been streamlined to a two-step process. The first step involves creating a key store database on both the client and server. The key store database manages your digital certificates used for SSL encryption (this is actually still done outside of DB2 using GSKit commands—but it's more integrated and easier to do). The second step involves setting the proper database manager configuration parameters on the server and client side, and any required connection attributes for the client, which varies depending on type. This second step is a one-time process on the server side, but it needs to be repeated for each client that is added in the future that you want to secure. Refer to the DB2 9.7 Information Center for details on how to configure SSL encryption in a DB2 environment.

Support for AES Encryption of User ID and Password

SSL encryption is used to encrypt all data that flows between the client and server. However, even if you're not interested in using the new SSL support to encrypt your complete database connection, you can still leverage the new AES algorithm to at least encrypt user IDs and passwords passed between the client and server. In this day and age, this is pretty much a given requirement for virtually all clients. You can use this encryption method for over-the-wire transfers of user IDs and passwords by specifying the `server_encrypt` authentication method using the following command:

```
UPDATE DATABASE MANAGER CONFIGURATION AUTHENTICATION server_encrypt;
```

When you've set this up, the exact choice of the encryption algorithm used, either DES or AES, will be decided by DB2 depending on what version of the client is connecting to the DB2 9.7 server and what encryption the client is requesting. This can be controlled by setting the `ALTERNATE_AUTH_ENC` database manager configuration parameter; if this parameter is set to `NOT_SPECIFIED` (the default), the server will accept whatever encryption algorithm that the client proposes. If set to `AES_CMP`, it will favor choosing AES when possible: even if the connecting client requests DES, DB2 will renegotiate and use AES encryption if the client supports it. Finally, setting this parameter to `AES_ONLY` means that the server will accept *only* AES encryption; if the client doesn't support AES encryption, the connection will be rejected.

5

The More Extensible DB2: pureXML Goes Crazy Scalable

The DB2 server's (referred to as DB2 in this chapter) pureXML capability was first introduced in the DB2 9 release. IBM chose the name pureXML for a specific reason—because DB2 actually stores and works with XML data in its purest format. pureXML treats XML data as a tree of XML elements and attributes and stores it that way, allowing faster insertion and retrieval of this semi-structured format. This approach differs from those taken by most of the other database vendors, who under the covers typically store the XML as a string of characters stuffed into a character large object (CLOB), or shred away the XML tags and store it relationally, or give you some mish-mash of choices that looks more like an appetizer menu. Of course, when you don't store your XML in a pure format like the one used by DB2, there's always a trade-off: typically, you need to choose one of two evils—a loss of performance or flexibility. The good news is that with DB2's pureXML, you never have to make such trade-offs.

IBM built, from the ground up, a pure native XML storage capability and reworked the DB2 engine into a hybrid engine that understands and processes both XML and relational data. It's called "pure" because the engineers didn't attempt to retrofit XML into the existing database infrastructure by mapping XML to relational concepts. Instead, they built a new *truly* native XML capability that works hand-in-hand with the existing infrastructure. By choosing such an approach, DB2 avoids many of the performance and flexibility (what XML is all about) hurdles that other vendors encounter. We've looked closely at our competitor's "native" XML technologies, and we're happy we called our technology pureXML. It's just that: pure.

Our last two books focused on DB2's industry-leading pureXML technology. In this chapter, we're assuming you're familiar with the "magic" behind the DB2 pureXML technology, so we'll focus on the enhancements that have taken pureXML to yet another inflection point as of DB2 9.7. If you're not familiar with pureXML, check out *The DB2 pureXML Cookbook* (http://ibmpressbooks.com/cookbook), co-authored by an individual we consider to be the King of XML, Matthias Nicola. Finally, we trust you are all aware that as of February 18, 2009, the pureXML technology available in DB2 is offered *free of charge for all DB2 editions* (it used to be a chargeable feature).

The headliner enhancement for pureXML in DB2 9.7 is that it now offers XML-based applications the near-linear DB2 scalability services, once solely reserved for relational data, through the DB2 partitioning services: Database Partitioning Feature (DPF), multidimensional clustering (MDC) tables, and table partitioning. (Note that InfoSphere Warehouse and the IBM Smart Analytics System is powered by the DB2 engine, and in this chapter references to DB2 refer either to DB2, InfoSphere Warehouse, or the IBM Smart Analytics System.) These scalability features are a gateway to the mainstream use of XML data as part of your business intelligence analytics strategy. DB2 9.7 also lets you compress the XML data area (XDA), the location where pureXML documents are stored if they are not inlined. DB2 9.5 allowed you to inline XML documents (and thus making them eligible for compression when part of the row). The XDA compression enhancements in DB2 9.7 enable XML documents to be compressed even if they are not inlined (this topic is covered in Chapter 1) as well as if they are inlined (from the work done in DB2 9.5).

pureXML and a Trifecta of DB2 Partitioning Options for Pure Scalability

Historically, the pureXML feature hasn't had a lot of use cases in a partitioned database environment. In DB2 9, pureXML wasn't even supported by DPF. DB2 9.5 included support for pureXML in DPF (though you likely didn't even know about it), but you had to put all the data on the catalog partition, and all the XML processing had to occur there as well. Consequently, the support of scaling-out pureXMLdata in DB2 9.5 wasn't really that useful in our opinion, since it really didn't scale out the processing.

As you're probably aware, as data volumes grow, distributing the contents of a database across multiple processors and storage devices can help you get as close to linear scalability as you can. In DB2 9.7, the DPF scalability services now fully support pureXML data. Using DPF, your XML data can be distributed across multiple database partitions, automatically parallelizing once long-running operations. In particular, these include internal operations associated with loading, inserting, querying, updating, deleting, validating, and publishing XML data. The key thing about XML and DPF, however, is its ability to parallelize complex analytical queries over XML data, which realistically slashes their response times roughly in proportion to the degree of parallelization. As with earlier releases of DB2, selecting a distribution key that evenly distributes rows across partitions is important. The distribution key must be based on a relational column. (It wouldn't make sense to distribute a row using an XML column as input into DB2's hashing algorithm.) We recommend you use the Design Advisor to help you identify an optimal distribution key for DPF based on your query workloads.

After you hash partition your data, each row of a given table (including the XML data) is placed in a specific database partition based on the hashed value of the table's distribution key, which is defined when the table is created. When data is read from or written to the database, DB2 automatically directs appropriate work to the relevant partitions that house the data. As a result, computing resources associated with multiple partitions may work in parallel to satisfy the original application's request. Near-linear scalability is achieved by adding new partitions as data volumes grow.

The extensions for XML and DPF in DB2 9.7 are really quite simple, since it's nearly identical to exploiting DPF for relational-only data in earlier releases. That is, a DBA simply leverages the appropriate database objects, such as partition groups, table spaces, buffer pools, and so on, and then creates the appropriate tables using the `DISTRIBUTE BY HASH` clause of the `CREATE TABLE` statement, as shown in Figure 5-1.

As you can see in Figure 5-1, DPF is a physical database design option that exploits "shared nothing" multiprocessing environments. It can be very useful for read-intensive workloads, including those common to data warehouse environments. The ability to scale-out XML processing however isn't just about performance of your queries; DPF can be used to scale out utility

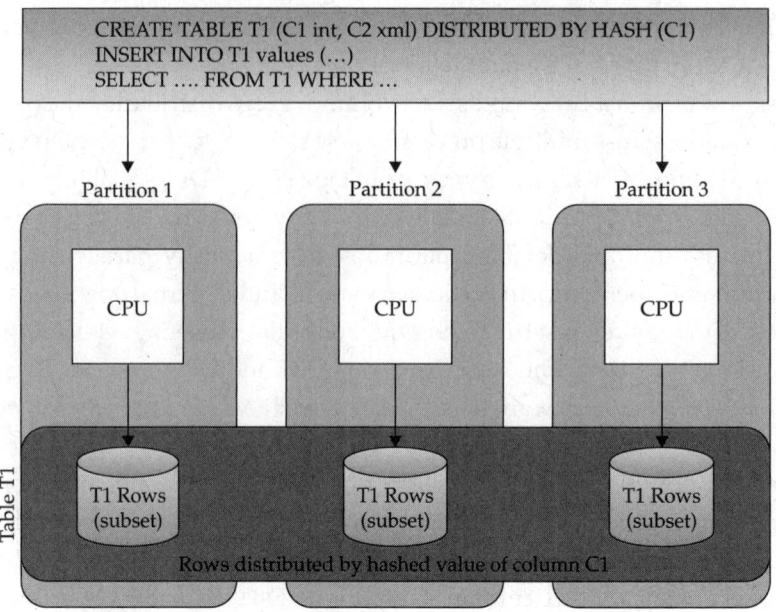

Figure 5.1 *pureXML data and hash partitioning*

performance and more. So it's a very powerful option and a cornerstone of very large database (VLDB) environments.

As you've likely figured out, DB2 has multiple partitioning capabilities, and they're all complimentary and synergize within their own key strengths to deliver unparalleled benefits to business intelligence (BI) workloads. DB2 9.7 really delivers a proven architecture for folding XML into BI. There are lots of opportunities here, from being able to search for unknown relationships in a bill of materials for supply chain optimization, to fluid star schemas that have dynamic XML-based dimensions around the Fact table, and *lots* more.

The DB2 DPF capability is primary a *scalability* feature. As shown in Figure 5-1, it parallelizes data across hashed partitions and delivers parallel query execution services as close as possible to where the data resides. The ability to mix DPF and XML together means that searched updates to XML data, construction of XML fragments, LOAD operations, and more can all be massively parallelized. Bottom line, your existing investment in DPF can now be leveraged for XML data as of DB2 9.7. If you're not using DPF today, now you've got even more reasons to use it as of DB2 9.7.

The More Extensible DB2: pureXML Goes Crazy Scalable

A frequent requirement for data warehouses and BI environments involves maintaining a rolling history of select data over a given period of time. For example, a firm might want to maintain a rolling five-year sales history so business analysts can assess buying patterns, evaluate emerging trends, and so on. In such a scenario, "old" data might need to be purged or archived on a monthly or quarterly basis, and current data might need to be loaded in a similar timeframe. *Table partitioning* is the DB2 technology that addresses this administrative requirement. Of course, table partitioning has performance benefits as well since the optimizer can intelligently perform predicate push down and branch tree elimination techniques to retrieve data quickly—but, in our opinion, table partitioning is about management, and the performance benefits (which get even better in DB2 9.7, as discussed in Chapter 2) are a nice by-product.

Table partitioning—sometimes called *range partitioning*—segments a table based on a range of values contained in one or more columns. Typically, a table partitioning key is time-based, resulting in a design that directs data for a given week, month, or quarter to be stored in a certain partition. Because each partition is treated as a separate database object, administrators can easily roll in (attach) new data or roll out (detach) old data. Before DB2 9.7, there was no support for pureXML and table partitioning (unlike DPF and pureXML). The good news is that DB2 9.7 delivers full support for pureXML and table partitioning. (As you logically expect, a pureXML column can't be used as part of the table partitioning key.)

Managing a range-partitioned table that includes one or more XML columns isn't much different from managing a range-partitioned table with only relational columns. In particular, the previously supported DDL statements

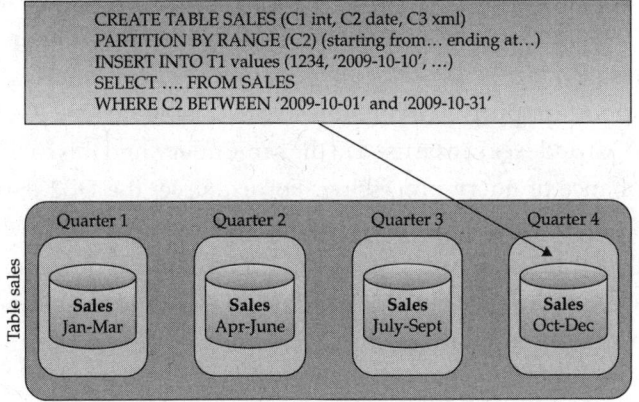

Figure 5.2 *pureXML data and table partitioning*

for creating and altering tables for range partitioning as well as attaching and detaching partitions still apply. To create a partitioned table that houses pureXML data, you leverage the same PARTITION BY RANGE clause that you've used since DB2 9, as shown in Figure 5-2.

Finally, DB2 9.7 supports the use of XML data within *MDC table dimensional partitioning*. As you're likely beginning to notice, you can't use an XML column as a dimensional clustering key. MDC tables are anything but new, but we are still baffled at the number of DBAs who aren't fully aware of their capabilities. DB2 9.7 enhances MDC table support with online space reclamation, but we also spent some time discussing the benefits of MDC tables in Chapter 1—so make sure you've read that chapter to learn about this BI panacea object.

Previous releases of DB2 supported the ability to cluster data dimensionally only if the table didn't have any pureXML columns. MDC tables are particularly useful for analytical applications, which typically issue queries spanning data contained in multiple columns. For example, an analytical application might require sales information contained in a large fact table table to be retrieved by product, region, and date (three dimensions). To support such a query, a DBA might use an MDC table to instruct DB2 to organize rows physically in the SALES table by these three dimensions. Because the rows related to sales for the same product in the same region and same time period would be co-located at the data page level, this design helps minimize I/O and significantly improves runtime performance of multidimensional queries. In addition, MDC tables also improve the performance of inserting and deleting data.

If you want XML columns to participate in multidimensional clustering, you use the ORGANIZE BY DIMENSION clause of the CREATE TABLE statement in that same manner that you would for tables with just relational data. Figure 5-3 illustrates a representation of an MDC table that contains pureXML column data.

With support for pureXML columns in MDC tables in DB2 9.7, both MDC block and XML indexes can be used in the same query, and this can really boost the performance of query processing. For example, the DB2 optimizer can generate INDEX ANDing plans for block indexes and use the XML value index to further optimize the retrieval of requested data. In addition, other MDC optimizations, such as fast block delete (fast roll-out) and fast block insert (fast roll-in) are all fully supported with XML data.

The More Extensible DB2: pureXML Goes Crazy Scalable

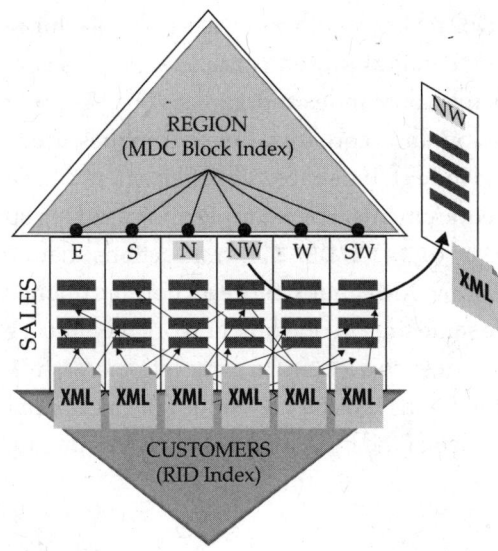

Figure 5.3 *MDC tables with XML data*

You can combine all the DB2 partitioning techniques for a synergistic effect that delivers unequaled manageability, scalability, and I/O optimization. Now mix in compression. We're getting excited!

Other pureXML Enhancements

In the remainder of this chapter, we'll detail some of the "not as flashy but still important enhancements" to the pureXML technology in DB2 9.7. These new pureXML features have some useful stuff that we want you to know about.

pureXML Gets More Online

Before DB2 9.7, you couldn't run a REORG INDEXES ALL FOR TABLE statement with the ALLOW WRITE ACCESS clause if the table had a pureXML column. In addition, you couldn't build a new index online using the CREATE INDEX statement. Quite simply, if the table had some defined relational indexes, then these indexes could not be reorganized since the relational indexes were in the same index object as the XML indexes.

As of DB2 9.7, DB2 no longer blocks writes to a table during online index reorganizations if XML data is present, and, as such, this new implementation closely resembles relational index reorganizations. As you might expect, the online index creation and reorganization techniques used by DB2 9.7 have some log space and index table space size requirements that are similar to their relational index requirements. For example, increased log space is needed for concurrent `INSERT/UPDATE/DELETE` transactions that are writing logical log records to a shadow XML index. Since all non-partitioned indexes must be reorganized at the same time in one unit of work, you must be sure to allocate adequate log space for such a `REORG` to complete successfully. In addition, online index reorganizations require an amount of free space in the index table space equal to the size of the index and the space needed to hold the shadow copy as well.

pureXML Gets More Programmatic

DB2 has long enabled application developers to create user-defined functions (UDFs) that can be invoked from queries. Creating such functions encourages code reuse and can simplify query development by incorporating code for commonly needed (and potentially complex) operations into a single module accessible to a variety of developers. Instead of hand-coding these operations into various queries, developers can simply call a function from each query that requires it. (Be sure to check out the new module and package support in DB2 9.7, which is bound to simplify the development of database business logic even more. We cover that in Chapter 6.)

DB2 9.7 now supports the XML data type in SQL-bodied and sourced UDFs. In addition, input and output parameters can be of type XML and UDFs that are written in SQL can include XML variables as well as SQL/XML statements. Writing UDFs that work with XML isn't much different from writing UDFs that work only with relational data types. The functions can be coded to return a single value (a scalar function) or multiple values (a table function). The latter can be particularly useful if you need to extract and return repeating elements from an XML document, such as a sequence of phone numbers or e-mail addresses for a given customer. For the DB2 9.7 release, compiled UDFs are not supported. Of course, DB2 9.7 continues to support using the XML data type in stored procedures, a capability first offered in an earlier release.

Support for Views Using XMLTABLE over XML

To support reporting software that doesn't fully handle XML data, the XMLTABLE function is a good workaround that should be included in your DBA bag of tricks. This function extracts values from an XML document and presents it to the application as a table of rows. The use of an XMLTABLE view requires that XML indexes be created on the underlying XML documents. Prior to DB2 9.7, some restrictions applied regarding the indexes you could exploit to speed up queries against such views, because of the semantic mismatch between SQL predicates and XQuery predicates. For example, SQL ignores trailing blanks and XML data can be un-typed, which is never the case in SQL, plus special values (such as +0, –0, –∞, and +∞) can be problematic.

As of DB2 9.7, you can also use XML indexes to support simple relational predicates on top of a view using an XMLTABLE function to extract the values.

Parallelized Bulk XML Decomposition

Although most of our writings about pureXML technology has been about why you want to keep XML data in the XML construct when storing it, in some use cases, you'll want to shred your XML into a relational format—for example, in an environment where the data will never be required to be returned in XML again and the environment processes data in the relational format. To support these use cases, DB2 9 shipped with a high-speed shredding capability called *XML decomposition*.

Keeping with the scalability theme of most of the DB2 9.7 pureXML enhancements, the DB2 decomposition services have been parallelized in DB2 9.7 so that they are even faster. Basically, new facilities can shred multiple XML documents at the same time. Previous releases of DB2 allowed you to declare only a single XML input document for each decomposition operation, which meant DB2 had to load the XML schema for each document, and then parse or serialize the document, one at a time. Now imagine having to do this for a million row table where each row has its own XML document and you can see just how much DB2 9.7 is going to help you.

In DB2 9.7, the new XDB_DECOMP_XML_FROM_QUERY system-supplied routine can take an existing DB2 table as input, effectively enabling DBAs to decompose data contained in a given column (there's also a command line method). For database designs that require shredding some or all of the contents of XML data, invocation of this routine can be particularly useful after a bulk load of XML documents into an XML or binary large object (BLOB) column. As with previous releases, DB2's decomposition facility relies on an annotated XML schema to map XML attributes and elements to specific columns of relational tables. (Note that a great graphical tool that's part of IBM Data Studio can help you generate an annotated schema.) Since DB2 supports XML schema flexibility, if multiple documents are validated against different schemas, but these schemas are all compatible, the latest version of the schema can be used to shred all the XML documents.

6

The More Compatible and Easier to Learn DB2

DB2 9.7 introduces a number of new features that will simplify development of SQL and SQL procedures. One of the challenges with SQL is that vendors tend to extend the capability of their products with features that are not part of the SQL standard. While one could suggest to developers that they should try to stick to existing standards, the reality is that many of these extensions are extremely useful and can significantly reduce development time.

In the case of DB2 9.7, a number of these new features are targeted at developers. By introducing new features, functions, tools, and utilities, developers familiar with other dialects of SQL can now use their existing skills against a DB2 server (referred to as DB2 in this chapter) database. This application flexibility gives customers more choices on what database platform to deploy on, rather than having their development teams being limited to just one database vendor. This approach allows businesses to maximize their human capital investment while at the same time enjoy the industry leading ROI that only DB2 can provide.

Break Free with DB2

DB2 9.7 includes a number of extensions to the database engine and utilities that will simplify application development, including the following:

- **Currently Committed** This new locking mechanism allows applications that read data from being locked by other applications updating data. In addition, any application that is reading data will not prevent another application from updating it.

- **New data types** NUMBER, VARCHAR2, TIMESTAMP, and DATE data types are new. In addition, the BOOLEAN data type has limited supported within procedures.

- **Time, math, and string functions** A large list of functions (string manipulation, date/time functions, and more) have been added the DB2 function list.

- **Non-standard SQL** Support for many extensions to SQL, including joins via the plus (+) operator, hierarchical queries, ROWNUM, and more.

- **PL/SQL (Procedural Language extensions to Structured Query Language)** Support for a subset of the Oracle database procedure language (PL/SQL) in procedures, functions, triggers, and as standalone statements.

- **Package support** The PACKAGE statement (MODULE in DB2) is now supported for easier development and grouping of database logic. This new object also facilitates easier deployment to other schemas or databases.

- **Package libraries in DB2** Several popular package libraries have been ported to DB2. These libraries add functionality to SQL, including capabilities for communicating through messages and alerts; creating, scheduling, and managing jobs; operating on large objects; executing dynamic SQL; working with files on the database server file system; sending e-mail; and more.

- **CLP Plus** A new command line processor (CLP), CLP Plus, provides support for creating, editing, and running SQL statements and scripts.

Enabling, Not Porting!

Prior to DB2 9.7, the amount of work it took to port an application from another database was heavily dependent on the amount of procedural code that was used. Issues would arise when non-standard features or functions would need to ported, sometimes requiring additional coding work.

The migration of an application would typically require six steps:

1. **Map schemas and data types**   Migrating schemas (tables, views, indexes, and so on) from another database to DB2 is relatively straightforward, although the use of certain nonstandard data types (such as VARCHAR2, MONEY, NUMBER) required some analysis of the application to make sure that the proper data type were used.

2. **Migrate data**   Once the schemas had been created, data migration was a relatively simple task.

3. **Translate programming objects**   This was the most labor-intensive portion of a migration. All the application objects, such as triggers, functions, and procedures, would need to be converted to native DB2. Tools were available to do much of this work, but a number of items could not be migrated without custom code written in Java or C, and this added a level of complexity to the migration.

4. **Translate SQL (applications)**   Applications that accessed the database needed to be migrated as well. The code would be examined for SQL to determine whether any of it would need to be changed. Syntax that was using SQL extensions (such as an outer join) would need to be rewritten. In some cases, the translation could not be accomplished by replacing the SQL. The application might need to have some of its logic reworked to work with DB2 semantics.

5. **Debug**   With the changes to application logic, the system would need more extensive debugging.

6. **Test and tune**   With the migration complete, the entire system would go through a testing and tuning cycle to ensure that the results matched the old system and that the performance was acceptable.

With the introduction of DB2 9.7, many of these steps have been shortened considerably, especially the application translation portion. Now, from a porting perspective, the steps have been simplified:

1. There is no need to map data types to DB2. Most data types used by other vendors are now supported natively in DB2.

2. Data migration can be done quickly without worrying about data type incompatibility.

3. Considerably less translation of database objects is required. DB2 now supports a subset of PL/SQL, so less workarounds are required.
4. DB2 supports many SQL extensions, so very few changes need to be made to an application.
5. Debugging is still required in any port of an application, but the amount of work should be considerably less.
6. Testing and tuning still need to be done to the application, but DB2 9.7's self-tuning features make this task much simpler.

In summary, DB2 9.7 gives the user the freedom to move from other databases to DB2 without incurring huge migration costs.

The DB2 Compatibility Vector

Many of the features discussed in this chapter aren't available unless the DB2 compatibility vector is used to turn on groups of compatibility features. You set the DB2 compatibility using the DB2SET command. For example, to enable all compatibility features in DB2 9.7, you will enter the following command:

DB2SET DB2_COMPATIBILITY_VECTOR=ORA.

NOTE: Some compatibility features were available in the DB2 9.5 release. In DB2 9.5, the DB2_COMPATABILITY setting to enable all features was FF. In DB2 9.7, this was changed to ORA; both settings enable the same features. However, we strongly recommend using the ORA setting, as new features could be added to subsequent releases, and the FFF setting may not enable them by default for compatibility reasons. Using ORA will ensure that any new features will be automatically enabled in the database.

You must understand that any change to DB2's compatibility vector requires that you recycle the instance *before* those changes take effect. In addition, you must create the database *after* the compatibility vector is set. This means that if you want to leverage most of the rich new compatibility features in DB2 9.7 in an existing database, you'll need to re-create the database. For example, assume you've created the DB2 SAMPLE database in DB2 9.5, but you now want to leverage all the new compatibility features in DB2 9.7. In this case, you'd have to issue the following commands:

```
DROP DATABASE SAMPLE;

DB2STOP FORCE;
!DB2SET DB2_COMPATIBILITY_VECTOR=ORA;
DB2START;
!DB2SAMPL -sql -xml;
```

In DB2 9.7, you can use any of the following DB2_COMPATIBILITY_VECTOR settings to enable a specific compatibility feature:

- **0x01**   Enables the use of ROWNUM as a synonym for ROW_NUMBER() OVER(), and permits ROWNUM to appear in the WHERE clause of an SQL statement.

- **0x02**   Resolves unqualified table references to DUAL as SYSIBM.DUAL.

- **0x04**   Enables support for the outer join operator (+).

- **0x08**   Enables support for hierarchical queries using the CONNECT BY clause.

- **0x10**   Enables the NUMBER data type and associated numeric processing.

- **0x20**   Enables the VARCHAR2 data type and associated character string processing.

- **0x40**   Enables use of the DATE data type as TIMESTAMP(0): a combined date and time value.

- **0x80**   Enables alternative semantics for the TRUNCATE TABLE statement, under which IMMEDIATE is an optional keyword that is assumed to be the default if not specified. An implicit commit operation is performed before the TRUNCATE statement executes if the TRUNCATE statement is not the first statement in the logical unit of work.

- **0x100**   Enables the assignment of the CHAR or GRAPHIC data type (instead of the VARCHAR or VARGRAPHIC data type) to character and graphic string constants whose byte length is less than or equal to 254. (This is often referred to as *character literals*.)

- **0x200** Enables the use of collection methods to perform operations on arrays, such as FIRST, LAST, NEXT, and PREVIOUS. This vector setting also enables the use of parentheses in place of square brackets in references to specific elements in an array; for example, array1(i) refers to element i of array1.
- **0x400** Enables the creation of data dictionary–compatible views.
- **0x800** Enables the compilation and execution of PL/SQL statements and language elements.

If you don't want to enable all the compatibility features, you've got the granular control to enable specific ones using their corresponding hexadecimal codes with the DB2_COMPATIBILITY_VECTOR registry variable. For example, you could enable just the DUAL and OUTER JOIN compatibility features for a DB2 database.

DB2 9.5 Compatibility Features

As mentioned, DB2 9.5 included some compatibility features when it became generally available, although we didn't talk about it much (perhaps we didn't want to let the cat out of the bag for what we had planned in DB2 9.7). Specifically, DB2 9.5 gave access to the following compatibility features that are also available in DB2 9.7: ROWNUM, DUAL, outer join (+), hierarchical query features, and the NUMBER and VARCHAR2 data types. A brief overview of these features is described next, while the new DB2 9.7 features are examined in detail in a separate section of this chapter.

ROWNUM

ROWNUM is a pseudo-value that can be used as an alternative to the DB2 FETCH FIRST <n> ROWS syntax that allows you to page through result sets. ROWNUM also maps to the ROW_NUMBER() OVER() function, which allows ROWNUM to be used in a WHERE clause rather than just in a SELECT statement.

The ROW_NUMBER (or ROWNUMBER) function computes the sequential row number of the row within the window defined by the ordering, starting with 1 for the first row. If the ORDER BY clause isn't specified in the window, the row numbers are assigned to the rows in an arbitrary order as returned by the SUBSELECT.

The following example numbers employee records returned, where the first employee has the highest salary:

```
SELECT ROWNUM, LASTNAME, SALARY FROM EMPLOYEE ORDER BY
SALARY DESC;

ROWNUM                 LASTNAME          SALARY
--------------------   ---------------   -----------
                   1   HAAS              152750.00
                   2   KWAN               98250.00
                   3   PULASKI            96170.00
                   4   THOMPSON           94250.00
                   5   HENDERSON          89750.00
                   6   SPENSER            86150.00
                   7   GEYER              80175.00
                   8   QUINTANA           73800.00
                   9   STERN              72250.00
                  10   JOHN               69840.00
```

Rather than using the FETCH FIRST N clause, the ROWNUM value can be used in the WHERE clause to limit output. The following SQL limits output to the first five rows from the EMPLOYEE table:

```
SELECT * FROM EMPLOYEE WHERE ROWNUM <= 5;

EMPNO    FIRSTNME       MIDINIT  LASTNAME   WORKDEPT  PHONENO
------   ------------   -------  ---------  --------  -------
000010   CHRISTINE      I        HAAS       A00       3978
000020   MICHAEL        L        THOMPSON   B01
000030   SALLY          A        KWAN       C01       4738
000050   JOHN           B        GEYER      E01
000060   IRVING         F        STERN      D11       6423
```

The ROWNUM operator could be used to limit the output of the SQL, but at the same time it also enumerates the rows that are being returned. Note that the ROWNUM in this SELECT statement refers to the position of the ROW in the final answer set, while the ROWNUM in the WHERE clause is the row number within the answer set:

```
SELECT ROWNUM, LASTNAME, SALARY
  FROM EMPLOYEE WHERE ROWNUM BETWEEN 5 AND 10 ORDER BY
SALARY DESC;

ROWNUM                 LASTNAME          SALARY
--------------------   ---------------   -----------
                   1   HENDERSON          89750.00
                   2   SPENSER            86150.00
```

```
          3 GEYER              80175.00
          4 QUINTANA           73800.00
          5 STERN              72250.00
          6 JOHN               69840.00
```

DUAL

The `DUAL` keyword is used in the same way that the DB2 `VALUES` is used. Its behavior is similar to that of `SYSDUMMY1`, except it doesn't require a qualifier. The `DUAL` keyword can be used to replace both the `VALUES` clause and the `SYSIBM.SYSDUMMY1` table schema; here's an example:

```
SELECT CURRENT DATE FROM DUAL;

1
-------------------
2009-07-05 00:27:43
```

Outer Join Operator

DB2 supports standard join syntax for left and right outer joins. Another popular syntax employs the (+) keyword to mark the *null-producing* column reference that precedes it in an implicit join notation. Specifically, the (+) keyword appears in the `WHERE` clause and refers to a column of the *inner* table in a *left outer join*. Here's an example:

```
SELECT * FROM T1, T2 WHERE T1.C1 = T2.C2 (+)
```

is the same as

```
SELECT * FROM T1 LEFT OUTER JOIN T2 ON T1.C1 = T2.C2
```

If you wanted to retrieve a list of departments and their employees, as well as the names of departments that have no employees, using the DB2 syntax, you'd use the following SQL statement:

```
SELECT DEPTNAME, LASTNAME
  FROM DEPARTMENT D LEFT OUTER JOIN EMPLOYEE E ON
  D.DEPTNO = E.WORKDEPT;

DEPTNAME                 LASTNAME
-------------------      ---------------
SPIFFY COMPUTER SERV     HAAS
PLANNING                 THOMPSON
INFORMATION CENTER       KWAN
SUPPORT SERVICES         GEYER
MANUFACTURING SYSTEM     STERN
```

```
ADMINISTRATION SYSTE  PULASKI
OPERATIONS            HENDERSON
SOFTWARE SUPPORT      SPENSER
SPIFFY COMPUTER SERV  LUCCHESSI
SPIFFY COMPUTER SERV  O'CONNELL
```

The following SQL statement example works in the same manner and retrieves the same data as the preceding statement; however, it uses the (+) syntax:

```
SELECT DEPTNAME, LASTNAME FROM DEPARTMENT D, EMPLOYEE E
  WHERE D.DEPTNO = E.WORKDEPT (+);
```

As you can see, this format is a lot simpler to remember than the OUTER JOIN syntax; however, remember that it isn't part of the SQL standard. Nevertheless, its simplicity has made it popular among many developers.

Hierarchical Queries

A hierarchical query allows a user to traverse relationships that are found within a table. This can be used to find routings (that is, going from one location to another), parts explosions (that is, all the parts that make up another part), and recursive relationships (that is, all departments that work under a particular manager). A form of a hierarchical query can be achieved with nested tables and UNION statements, which doesn't require temporary tables in order to work.

To illustrate this feature, run the following data definition language (DDL) code, which creates the EMPL table that contains a list of employees and their respective manager's employee number:

```
CREATE TABLE EMPL
   (NAME VARCHAR(15),
    EMPID INT NOT NULL PRIMARY KEY,
    MGRID INT);
INSERT INTO EMPL VALUES
('Alyse',1,NULL),('Paul',2,1),('Belal',3,2),
('Chris',4,2),('Dwaine',5,1),('Bob',6,5),
('Kevin',7,6),('Jim',8,6),('George',9,6);
```

The following hierarchical query returns all employees who work for Alyse (either directly reporting to her or indirectly reporting to her through a manager that reports to her directly):

```
SELECT EMPL.*, SUBSTR(SYS_CONNECT_BY_PATH
 (TRIM(CHAR(EMPID)),':'),1,20)
```

```
        AS PATH FROM EMPL START WITH NAME='Alyse'
        CONNECT BY PRIOR EMPID = MGRID;

NAME                 EMPID           MGRID           PATH
---------------      ----------      ----------      -----------------
Alyse                    1               -           :1
Paul                     2               1           :1:2
Belal                    3               2           :1:2:3
Chris                    4               2           :1:2:4
Dwaine                   5               1           :1:5
Bob                      6               5           :1:5:6
Kevin                    7               6           :1:5:6:7
Jim                      8               6           :1:5:6:8
George                   9               6           :1:5:6:9
```

Of course, you could get the same query results using a nested table expression that's been available in DB2 for some time, but these expressions are considerably more tedious to write.

The NUMBER Data Type

The NUMBER data type is a synonym for DECFLOAT or DECIMAL depending on whether a precision or scale is used. When the NUMBER data type is explicitly used in a SQL statement, it is implicitly mapped as follows:

- If NUMBER is specified without precision and scale attributes, it is mapped to DECFLOAT(16).
- If NUMBER(p) is specified, it is mapped to DECIMAL(p).
- If NUMBER(p,s) is specified, it is mapped to DECIMAL(p,s).

All operations on DECIMAL and DECFLOAT data types are done in DECFLOAT(34) to maintain the highest precision for the operation; trailing zeros are stripped out during string conversion (also referred to as *normalization*).

When you use the NUMBER data type in a DB2 9.7 database, that database becomes locked into this newly supported behavior to prevent anomalies in the stored data. The following DDL creates a table with the NUMBER data type and populates it with data:

```
CREATE TABLE NUMBERTEST
  (SALARY NUMBER, BONUS NUMBER(5,2), COMMISSION DECIMAL(13,4));
```

```
INSERT INTO NUMBERTEST VALUES
  (1452.430,123.33,1452.430),(1562.0000,555.22,1562.0000),
  (1.55555,144.22,1.55555);
```

The NUMBER data type—and DECFLOAT for that matter—doesn't normally need you to specify its precision explicitly after the decimal place. This data type keeps a total of 16 significant digits, regardless of the number of digits that appear after the decimal place in the data. You should also be aware that trailing zeros are *always* dropped when the number is converted to a string. Use the following SELECT statement to see how the data inserted in the preceding example is stored in the database:

```
SELECT * FROM NUMBERTEST;

SALARY             BONUS    COMMISSION
---------------    -------  ---------------
        1452.43    123.33        1452.4300
           1562    555.22        1562.0000
        1.55555    144.22           1.5556
```

The VARCHAR2 Data Type

The VARCHAR2 data type is a synonym for DB2's VARCHAR data type. VARCHAR2 can be used as a data type directly in a CREATE TABLE statement. VARCHAR2 has the same storage characteristics as the VARCHAR data type, but it has slightly different semantics, mostly due to the way that NULLs are handled with a character string stored in a VARCHAR2 column.

The following example creates the TESTVARCHAR2 table that contains a VARCHAR2 and VARCHAR column; both of these data types are equivalent when you turn the compatibility vector on.

```
CREATE TABLE TESTVARCHAR2
  (COL1 VARCHAR2(255), COL2 VARCHAR(255));
```

As mentioned, the majority of differences between VARCHAR2 and VARCHAR data types involve the handling of NULLs. In DB2, inserting an empty string into a VARCHAR column results in an empty string being inserted into the table; however, inserting the same empty string into a VARCHAR2 column results in a NULL value. Try it for yourself using the following example:

```
INSERT INTO TESTVARCHAR2 VALUES ('','');
```

```
SELECT DECODE(COL1, NULL,'Null','Not Null') FROM
TESTVARCHAR2;


1
--------
Null
```

With a VARCHAR2 column, a substring that's outside the range of the character string being modified will return a NULL value as opposed to an empty string, as shown in the following example, which builds upon the preceding example:

```
DELETE FROM TESTVARCHAR2;
INSERT INTO TESTVARCHAR2 VALUES
(SUBSTR('Hello',1,0),'');
SELECT DECODE(COL1, NULL,'Null','Not Null') FROM
TESTVARCHAR2;

1
--------
Null
```

You should also be aware that concatenation of NULLs is different with the VARCHAR2 data type. For example, if you concatenate using a NULL with the normal DB2 semantics, the result will be a NULL; however, if you do this with the new VARCHAR2 data type, the original string will be returned, as shown here:

```
VALUES
  'Hello' || CAST(NULL AS VARCHAR(1))
1
------
Hello
```

The way that strings with trailing blanks are compared is very similar between the VARCHAR2 and VARCHAR data types. In the following example, both strings end up being equal, even though there are trailing blanks:

```
VALUES
  .CASE
      WHEN 'Hello' = 'Hello    ' THEN 'True'
      ELSE 'Hello' <> 'Hello    ' THEN 'False'
   END
1
-----
True
```

While constants have their trailing blanks removed during comparisons, the same is not true for values inserted into a table with the VARCHAR2 data type. In the following example, the TESTVARCHAR2 table has two VARCHAR2 columns to help demonstrate comparison operators with this data type. A value of `'Hello'` is inserted into column 1, while `'Hello '` (note the extra space) is inserted into the second table. If you run some SQL to compare both columns, you'll find that they are different, as shown next:

```
DELETE FROM TESTVARCHAR2;

INSERT INTO TESTVARCHAR2 VALUES ('Hello','Hello   ');

SELECT COL1, COL2,
   CASE
      WHEN COL1=COL2  THEN 'Equal'
      WHEN COL1<>COL2 THEN 'Not Equal'
   END
FROM TESTVARCHAR2

COL1                   COL2                    3
-------------------    -------------------     ---------
Hello                  Hello                   Not Equal
```

The New DB2 9.7 Compatibility Features

DB2 9.7 takes compatibility to a whole new level by providing support for many of the most commonly used extensions to SQL. The remainder of this chapter details the new features added in DB2 9.7.

Parameterized Timestamps

A timestamp is a seven-part value that consists of year, month, day, hour, minute, second, and microsecond that designates a date and time and includes a fractional specification of microseconds. The complete string representation of a timestamp has the form `yyyy-mm-dd-hh.mm.ss.nnnnnn`, while the internal representation of a timestamp is a string of 10 bytes. Each byte consists of two packed decimal digits. The first 4 bytes represent the date, the next 3 bytes the time, and the last 3 bytes the microseconds.

Prior to DB2 9.7, a timestamp always included six digits of microsecond accuracy. Sometimes this additional precision was not required, and sometimes it did not offer enough. In DB2 9.7, the TIMESTAMP data type now allows for parameterized precision by including a range of 0 (no fractional seconds) to 12 (picoseconds).

The DB2 9.7 capability to allow parameterization of TIMESTAMP columns has two main benefits. First, the increased precision improves the granularity and power of the TIMESTAMP data type. Second, the TIMESTAMP data becomes more flexible since it can be adjusted to match the requirements of the application. For example, if an application requires only data and time values, a TIMESTAMP defined with precision of 0 would save 3 bytes per row versus the default implementation. This is yet another way that DB2 9.7 optimizes the on-disk footprint of your database beyond compression (we discussed these methods in Chapter 1).

The DATE Data Type

DB2 supported the DATE data type well before DB2 9.7. This data type normally comprises the year, month, and day. However, by setting the DB2_COMPATIBLITY_VECTOR=40, or by enabling DB2 to support all compatibility features via the ORA setting, you can force DB2 to interpret the DATE data type as a TIMESTAMP(0) data type. A TIMESTAMP(0) data type comprises the year, month, day, hour, minute, and second.

Before the aforementioned flexibility of the TIMESTAMP data type as of DB2 9.7, an application that needed both time and date values would have to use separate TIME and DATE fields or resort to using static TIMESTAMP data type. Of course, using two fields can present some extra work if you need to perform any date/time arithmetic. One workaround could have been to use a TIMESTAMP column, but that data type uses significantly more storage. As of DB2 9.7, with the introduction of parameterized timestamps, a DATE field can now simulate a TIMESTAMP(0) data type. The DB2 9.7 DATE data type includes the year, month, and day along with the hours and seconds components; if your application requires more granularity, a TIMESTAMP field could be used.

Friendly Date Arithmetic

With the addition of the new DATE data type, the rules for assigning TIMESTAMP values to a date field have been relaxed compared to previous versions of DB2. For example, prior to DB2 9.7, a TIMESTAMP needed to be converted to a proper DATE format using one of the built-in date functions. In

DB2 9.7, a TIMESTAMP can be directly assigned to a DATE field, which provides a lot of flexibility and less effort for your applications:

```
DROP TABLE DATEXMP;

CREATE TABLE DATEXMP(ADATE DATE);

INSERT INTO DATEXMP VALUES(CURRENT TIMESTAMP);

SELECT * FROM DATEXMP;

ADATE
------------------
2009-07-05 00:27:45
```

Truncate Table

For a while, clients have asked for a "quick delete" feature in DB2. In most circumstances, record deletions from a table should be logged. For example, in the event of a system failure or transaction rollback, having the previous image of the row is critical for recovery. However, in some circumstances, such as deleting a range of sales data in a partitioned table, large amounts of data need to be removed from a table and logging this event isn't important to the integrity of the database.

Dropping a table was one alternative for removing all the records. While this was quick, it caused numerous issues with application objects and security that relied on this table. All the existing definitions on the table are lost when it is dropped, so all objects would need to be re-created if you used this method. Other non-standard ways of removing data without logging could be used, but none of them used standard SQL facilities.

In DB2 9.7, a new TRUNCATE TABLE command allows for the massive deletion of rows *without* causing any logging. This new command has multiple benefits—most notably, faster performance over traditional deletion of rows. The syntax of the TRUNCATE table command is TRUNCATE TABLE <*table_name*> [*Options*] IMMEDIATE.

The TRUNCATE TABLE command always runs immediately and must be the first statement in a unit of work (UOW). Use caution when using this command, because it doesn't perform any recovery logging for the data, so this operation can't be rolled back and your data will be gone. Quite simply, a truncated table is immediately available after the statement completes, but a

ROLLBACK statement can't roll back the truncate operation and the table remains in a truncated state. So, for example, if another data change operation occurs on the table after a TRUNCATE IMMEDIATE statement, and then a ROLLBACK statement is run, the processed table truncation won't be undone, even though all other data change operations are undone.

The TRUNCATE TABLE command supports the following options:

- **DROP/REUSE STORAGE** Tells DB2 to release the storage previously occupied by the table back to the operating system. In many cases, the table will be reloaded with data, so you may want to keep the storage.

- **IGNORE DELETE TRIGGERS or RESTRICT WHEN DELETE TRIGGERS** Tells DB2 not to fire any triggers during the TRUNCATE TABLE command or instructs DB2 not to truncate the table unless the DELETE triggers have been removed.

- **CONTINUE IDENTITY** Instructs DB2 to continue using the IDENTITY values in the table from where it last left off before the truncate operation completed.

NOTE: Ignoring DELETE triggers can result in inconsistent results in tables that are dependent on the base table.

Character Literals

This feature enables the assignment of the CHAR or GRAPHIC data type (instead of the VARCHAR or VARGRAPHIC data type) to character and graphic string constants whose byte length is less than or equal to 254.

Collection Methods

Enabling this compatibility feature allows DB2 to perform operations on arrays such as FIRST, LAST, NEXT, and PREVIOUS. More importantly, this value enables the use of parentheses in place of square brackets in references to specific elements in an array. The following example uses the standard DB2 syntax to define an array type and populate it with values:

```
CREATE PROCEDURE ARRAY_XMP
   LANGUAGE SQL
BEGIN
```

```
    DECLARE SALARIES SALARY;
    DECLARE I INTEGER DEFAULT 0;

    WHILE I <= 5 DO
       SET SALARIES[I] = I;
    END WHILE;
END;
/
```

Note that the [ ] brackets in the code can be replaced with ( ) instead:

```
SET SALARIES(I) = I;
```

Data Dictionary-Compatible Views

DB2 does not contain tables that describe database metadata. Applications written for other databases depend on data dictionaries, so a new feature was added to DB2 9.7 to support a database metadata view. Data dictionary–compatible view support can be enabled through the DB2_COMPATIBILITY_VECTOR registry variable. When this registry variable is set to support these views, they will be automatically created when the database is created. The data dictionary views are self-describing. The DICTIONARY view returns a listing of all data dictionary views with comments that describe the content of each view. The DICT_COLUMNS view returns a list of all columns in all data dictionary views. With these two views, you can determine what information is available and how to access it.

Up to three different versions of each data dictionary view are available (each is identified by the prefix of the view name). Each view returns information about the database objects, specifically the following information:

- USER_* views return information about objects that are owned by the current database user.

- ALL_* views return information about objects to which the current user has access.

- DBA_* views return information about all objects in the database, regardless of who owns them.

These views can be further categorized into four sections: general, tables or views, programming objects, and security. Each category has literally dozens of views. For example, general views include DICTIONARY, DICT_COLUMNS

USER_CATALOG, DBA_CATALOG, ALL_CATALOG USER_DEPENDENCIES, and more. Refer to the DB2 documentation for information.

The data dictionary views can be used like any other object within DB2. To list the contents of the dictionary, enter the following SQL:

```
SELECT * FROM DICTIONARY;
```

TABLE_SCHEMA	TABLE_NAME	COMMENTS
SYSIBMADM	DBA_ARGUMENTS	Arguments in all…
SYSIBMADM	ALL_ARGUMENTS	Arguments in objects
SYSIBMADM	USER_ARGUMENTS	Arguments in objects
SYSIBMADM	DBA_CATALOG	All database tables,
SYSIBMADM	ALL_CATALOG	All accessible table
SYSIBMADM	USER_CATALOG	All users own table
SYSIBMADM	DBA_COL_COMMENTS	Comments on columns
SYSIBMADM	ALL_COL_COMMENTS	Comments on columns
SYSIBMADM	USER_COL_COMMENTS	Comments on columns
SYSIBMADM	DBA_CONS_COLUMNS	Information about…

If you want to see all database tables, you can query the ALL_TABLES view. If you want to see only the tables created by the current user, use the USER_ prefix:

```
SELECT * FROM USER_TABLES;
```

TABLE_SCHEMA	TABLE_NAME	TABLESPACE_NAME	PCT_FREE
BAKLARZ	T1	SESSIONTEMP	-1
BAKLARZ	ACT	USERSPACE1	-1
BAKLARZ	ADEFUSR	USERSPACE1	-1
BAKLARZ	CL_SCHED	USERSPACE1	-1
BAKLARZ	DEPARTMENT	USERSPACE1	-1

PL/SQL Compilation

PL/SQL compilation is perhaps the most important compatibility option of all the features you can select individually using the DB2_COMPATIBILITY_ VECTOR. As its name implies, this feature turns on the PL/SQL support within the DB2.

When you turn on PL/SQL compilation support for a DB2 9.7 database, you can use a subset of PL/SQL when creating, replacing, or dropping a wide range of objects including anonymous blocks, functions, packages, package bodies, routines, triggers, and more. In addition, this feature supports many of the PL/SQL logic statements including the following:

- Type declarations (supported within packages)
- Associative arrays, record types, and VARRAY types
- Variable declarations (%ROWTYPE, %TYPE, and so on)
- Statements (assignment statements, NULL statements, the RETURNING INTO clause)
- Statement attributes (SQL%FOUND, SQL%NOTFOUND, and SQL%ROWCOUNT)
- Control statements (simple CASE statement, searched CASE statement, exception handling, EXIT, FOR, GOTO, IF, LOOP, WHILE)
- Static cursors (CLOSE, CURSOR FOR LOOP statement, FETCH, FETCH INTO, OPEN, parameterized cursors, cursor attributes)
- REF CURSOR support (variables and parameters of type REF CURSOR, strong REF CURSORs, OPEN FOR statement, returning REF CURSORs to JDBC applications)
- Error support (RAISE_APPLICATION_ERROR, RAISE statement, SQLCODE function, SQLERRM function)

DB2 accepts PL/SQL input natively. Developers don't need to translate the PL/SQL into an intermediate dialect or use a separate program to import the information into DB2. By turning on DB2's PL/SQL compatibility support, DB2 compiles the PL/SQL *natively* into executable code in the DB2 engine, without going through an interpretive stage, as shown in Figure 6-1.

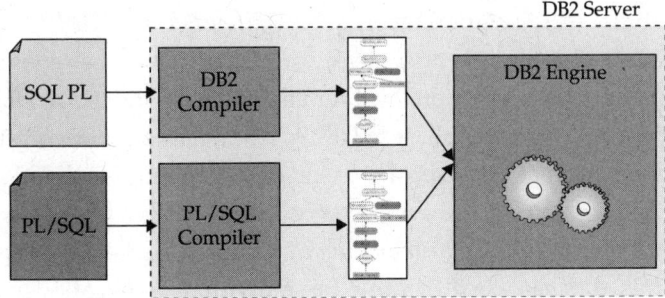

Figure 6.1 *The PL/SQL support in DB2 9.7 is native, not emulation.*

The BOOLEAN Data Type

The BOOLEAN data type isn't a data type you use in the creation of a table; instead, it's a new system-defined type for use within applications because it provides support for declaring and referencing the system-defined logical values TRUE, FALSE, and NULL within compound SQL (compiled) statements. The BOOLEAN data type can be assigned values and used in expressions like any other data type. For example, the following code creates a BOOLEAN data type and assigns it a value of TRUE:

```
BEGIN
  DECLARE BUYDB2 BOOLEAN;
  CALL DBMS_OUTPUT.PUT_LINE('BUY DB2=' ||
     DECODE(BUYDB2,TRUE,'True',FALSE,'False','Undecided'));
  SET BUYDB2 = TRUE;
  CALL DBMS_OUTPUT.PUT_LINE('BUY DB2=' ||
     DECODE(BUYDB2,TRUE,'True',FALSE,'False','Undecided'));
END;
/

BUY DB2=Undecided
BUY DB2=True
```

You can't get the value of a BOOLEAN data type using the DBMS_OUTPUT routine; instead, as shown in the preceding example, a DECODE or CASE statement should be used to convert the BOOLEAN value into something more meaningful.

Currently Committed: Readers Don't Block Writers. Writers Don't Block Readers.

DB2 9.7 introduces a new locking isolation level that's built on and extends the Cursor Stability (CS) isolation level called *Currently Committed (CC)*. The CC isolation level significantly reduces lock wait and deadlock scenarios and is the new default databases isolation level for any database created in DB2 9.7 and beyond. If you upgrade a database to DB2 9.7, the old isolation level remains the default to ensure that expected behavior doesn't change unless you say it does—which you can do using the CUR_COMMIT database configuration parameter that specifies the default locking mechanism for the database. You can override this database-level setting for individual applications using the CONCURRENTACCESSRESOLUTION option of the BIND and PRECOMPILE commands. You override this database-level setting for stored procedures using the

`DB2_SQLROUTINE_PREPOPTS` registry variable and the `SET_ROUTINE_OPTS` procedure. Currently committed semantics apply only to read-only scans that do not involve catalog tables or the internal scans that are used to evaluate constraints.

Before DB2 9.7, an application running the CS isolation level could wait while a row that was being updated (writers blocked readers) until the transaction was completed. Let's look at a potential locking problem that's likely to occur using the default isolation level prior to DB2 9.7. In this example, you work in the Human Resources (HR) department and use an HR application to process an employee's promotion, and this implicitly increases her salary. The HR application therefore issues SQL similar to the following:

```
UPDATE EMPLOYEE SET SALARY = 40000 WHERE EMPNO = 5;
```

Simultaneously, another HR partner uses the HR application to update the new location of a new branch office, and that operation results in SQL similar to the following:

```
UPDATE DEPARTMENT SET LOCATION='ROCKWOOD' WHERE DEPTNO='A501';
```

At this point, you try to retrieve location information about a department and at the same time a request is made for details by another HR partner on the details of an employee. These operations result in two SQL statements that hit the database server and look like this:

```
SELECT LOCATION FROM DEPARTMENT WHERE DEPTNO='A501';
SELECT * FROM EMPLOYEE WHERE EMPNO = 5;
```

If you try this example for yourself (assuming your database isn't set to `AUTOCOMMIT` transactions), you're going to find that it results in a classic deadlock condition. The first transaction can't complete because it's waiting for the lock on the DEPARTMENT table to be released. At the same time, the second transaction can't finish because it's waiting for locks on the EMPLOYEE table to be released. To solve this problem prior to DB2 9.7, a deadlock victim algorithm would roll back one of the transactions.

The new DB2 9.7 CC isolation level will handle this scenario very differently: Both transactions would complete successfully! In the case of the first transaction, the user would have received the location of the department prior to the update, while the second transaction would have received information about the employee before the increase in salary.

PL/SQL Packages in DB2

A PL/SQL package is a named collection of functions, procedures, variables, cursors, user-defined types (UDTs), and records that are referenced using a common qualifier: the *package name*. Packages have the following characteristics and benefits:

- **Convenient organization**   Packages provide a convenient way of organizing the functions and procedures that have a related purpose.

- **Simplified security**   Permissions to use the functions and procedures within the package are dependent on one privilege that is granted to the entire package. This makes administration a lot simpler than having to GRANT use of each function and object that makes up a package.

- **Public entities**   Selected items within a package can be declared PUBLIC. Public entities are visible and can be referenced by other programs that hold the EXECUTE privilege on the package. The code for the functions and procedures that make up the package are not accessible to others. This helps implement the principle of least privilege.

- **Private entities**   Other items in a package can be declared PRIVATE and can be referenced only by functions and procedures within the package.

An example of a package declaration is shown next:

```
CREATE OR REPLACE PACKAGE customer_admin
IS
    FUNCTION get_cust_name (
        p_custno        NUMBER
    )
    RETURN VARCHAR2;
    FUNCTION get_cust_phone (
        p_custno        NUMBER,
    )
    RETURN NUMBER;
    PROCEDURE add_customer(
        p_custno        NUMBER,
        p_name          VARCHAR2,
        p_address       VARCHAR2,
        p_phone         NUMBER
    );
    PROCEDURE drop_customer (
        p_custno        NUMBER
    );
END customer_admin;
```

Package Libraries in DB2

DB2 9.7 provides a number of system-defined modules of package libraries that provide a programmatic interface for performing a variety of useful operations. These modules can be invoked from an SQL-based application, the DB2 command line, or a command script. The following modules (packages) are currently supported:

- **DBMS_ALERT** Provides a set of procedures for registering alerts, sending alerts, and receiving alerts.
- **DBMS_JOB** Provides procedures for the creation, scheduling, and managing of jobs.
- **DBMS_LOB** Provides the capability to operate on large objects (LOBs).
- **DBMS_OUTPUT** Provides a set of procedures for putting messages (lines of text) in a message buffer and getting messages from it, too. These procedures are useful during application debugging when you need to write messages to standard output.
- **DBMS_PIPE** Provides a set of routines for sending messages through a pipe within or between sessions that are connected to the same database.
- **DBMS_SQL** Provides a set of procedures for executing dynamic SQL and therefore supports various Data Manipulation Language (DML) or data definition language (DDL) statements.
- **DBMS_UTILITY** Provides various utility programs.
- **UTL_DIR** Provides a set of routines for maintaining directory aliases that are used with the UTL_FILE module.
- **UTL_FILE** Provides a set of routines for reading from and writing to files on the database server's file system.
- **UTL_MAIL** Provides the capability to send e-mail.
- **UTL_SMTP** Provides the capability to send e-mail over the Simple Mail Transfer Protocol (SMTP).

One of the often requested extensions to DB2 procedural language is the ability to print debugging information from within a procedure. Prior to DB2 9.7, diagnostic information could not be produced without using intermediate tables. In DB2 9.7, the `DBMS_OUTPUT` module can be used to produce output, as shown here:

```
BEGIN
  DBMS_OUTPUT.PUT_LINE('Hello World');
END;
/
```

```
Hello World
```

Each package library has multiple functions and procedures that can be called from within SQL (as shown), from the DB2 command line, or from a script and used by your applications. These functions and procedures extend the type of work that you can do directly from the DB2 environment.

CLP Plus

The Command Line Processor Plus (CLP Plus) is a new, easy to use, interactive CLP for SQL statements and database commands. CLP Plus provides a command line UI from which you can connect to databases, and develop, edit, and execute SQL statements, SQL Procedural Language (SQL PL) statements, PL/SQL statements, scripts, and commands related to the operating system and database management. The features of CLP Plus include the following:

- Interactive CLI.
- Support for managing connections to databases when a database user ID and password are provided.
- A buffer that can be used to store scripts, script fragments, SQL statements, SQL PL statements, or PL/SQL statements for editing and subsequent execution. Text in the buffer can be listed, printed, edited, or run as a batch script.
- A comprehensive set of processor commands can be used to define variables, strings, and text elements that can be stored in the buffer.
- A set of commands that retrieve information about the database and database objects.

- Ability to store buffers or buffer output to a file.
- Multiple options for formatting the output of scripts and queries.
- Support for executing system-defined routines.
- Support for executing operating system commands.
- Option for recording the output of executed commands, statements, or scripts.

A sample CLP Plus screen is shown in Figure 6-2.

In addition to CLP Plus, the CLP has been enhanced to support the use of the slash character (/) as the terminator for PL/SQL statements. To turn on this feature, use the SET SQLCOMPAT PLSQL command in the script before issuing CREATE, DECLARE, or BEGIN statements that use semicolons as delimiters:

```
SET SQLCOMPAT PLSQL;
CREATE OR REPLACE PROCEDURE TEST(...)
BEGIN
  ...
END;
/
  SET SQLCOMPAT DB2;
```

To set the behavior of semicolons back to normal, issue the SET SQLCOMPAT DB2 command.

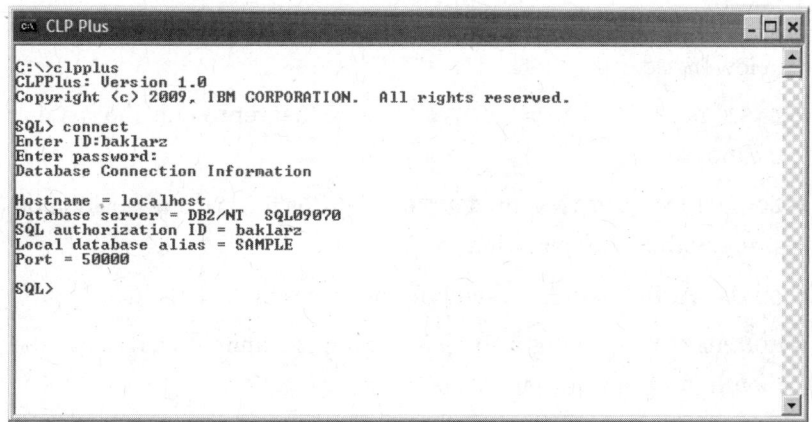

Figure 6.2 *CLP Plus*

New and Improved Scalar Functions

Following are some of the many new and improved scalar functions in DB2 9.7:

- **ADD_MONTHS**   Returns a `DATETIME` value that represents an expression plus a specified number of months.
- **ARRAY_DELETE**   Deletes elements from an array.
- **ARRAY_FIRST**   Returns the smallest array index value of the array.
- **ARRAY_LAST**   Returns the largest array index value of the array.
- **ARRAY_NEXT**   Returns the next largest array index value for an array relative to the specified array index argument.
- **ARRAY_PRIOR**   Returns the next smaller array index value for an array relative to the specified array index argument.
- **CURSOR_ROWCOUNT**   Returns the cumulative count of all rows fetched by the specified cursor since the cursor was opened.
- **DAYNAME**   Returns a character string containing the name of the day (for example, Friday).
- **DECFLOAT_FORMAT (TO_NUMBER)**   Converts a string to a DECFLOAT data type.
- **EXTRACT**   Returns a portion of a date or timestamp.
- **INITCAP**   Takes a string expression and returns a string expression with the first character of each word in uppercase and all other letters in lowercase.
- **LAST_DAY**   Returns a `DATETIME` value that represents the last day of the month.
- **LOCATE_IN_STRING or INSTR**   Returns the starting position of a string within another string.
- **LPAD**   Adds characters, symbols, or spaces to the left side of a string.
- **MONTHNAME**   Returns a character string containing the name of the month (for example, January).

- **MONTHS_BETWEEN** Returns an estimate of the number of months between two expressions.
- **NEXT_DAY** Returns a DATETIME value that represents the first weekday later than the date in a specified expression.
- **ROUND_TIMESTAMP** Returns a timestamp value from an expression rounded to a specified unit.
- **RPAD** Adds characters, symbols, or spaces to the right of a string.
- **TO_CLOB or CLOB** Converts character data to the CLOB data type.
- **TO_NUMBER or DECFLOAT_FORMAT** Returns a DECFLOAT(34) value that is based on the interpretation of a string using the specified format.
- **TO_TIMESTAMP or TIMESTAMP_FORMAT** Returns a timestamp that is based on the interpretation of a string using the specified format.
- **TRIM_ARRAY** Deletes elements from the end of an array.
- **TRUNC_TIMESTAMP** Adds characters, symbols, or spaces to the right side of a string.

Any of these functions can be used within a SQL statement. Here's an example:

```
VALUES INITCAP('capitalize the first letter of each word');
1
-----------------------------------------------
Capitalize The First Letter Of Each Word
```

Public Synonyms

In previous versions of DB2, an alias or synonym was an alternative name for a nickname, table, view, or another alias. It could be used to reference an object wherever that object can be referenced directly. For example, the following statement creates an alias for the table BAKLARZ.TRANSACTIONS:

```
CREATE ALIAS TXS FOR BAKLARZ.TRANSACTIONS;
```

Whenever an application needs to access the base table, it can do so by substituting the alias name instead. The following procedure returns the count of records in the TXS table:

```
CREATE OR REPLACE PROCEDURE COUNT_TXS()
  BEGIN
    DECLARE I INTEGER DEFAULT 0;

    SET I = (SELECT COUNT(*) FROM TXS);
    CALL DBMS_OUTPUT.PUT_LINE('COUNT=' || VARCHAR(I));
  END;
/

CALL COUNT_TXS();

COUNT=10000
```

At a later date, you could change the alias to a different value. For example, perhaps you're moving an application from the quality control phase to production; rather than modifying the source code, only the alias would need to be changed. Here's an example:

```
CREATE OR REPLACE ALIAS TXT FOR BAKLARZ.EMPLOYEE;

CALL COUNT_TXS();

COUNT=42
```

Normally, you would change an alias to point to a similar table; otherwise, any routines that depended on it would fail. DB2 9.7 extends the alias functionality to support modules and sequences in addition to the existing support for tables, views, and nicknames. You should be aware, however, that you can't use aliases in the CHECK condition of a CHECK CONSTRAINT and aliases can't reference declared global temporary tables (although they can reference the new to DB2 9.7 created global temporary tables).

The alias that was created in the preceding example is considered a *local alias*—or, more specifically, it's an *alias associated with a schema*. The reference to TXS in this procedure was implicitly referring to the full qualified name BAKLARZ.TXS. To create an alias that has a global reach across all schemas in the database, the PUBLIC keyword needs to be added to the CREATE ALIAS command. The following example illustrates this concept:

```
CREATE PUBLIC ALIAS TXS FOR BAKLARZ.EMPLOYEE;
```

The COUNT_TXS procedure will continue to work but now uses the public alias TXS.

Implicit Casting

Implicit casting is a technique that allows data types to be compared or assigned even if they are different types. Before DB2 9.7, all assignments required strong typing, which meant that both data types must be converted to a common type before the assignment could be accomplished. In DB2 9.7, application development gets a lot easier, because, rather than raising an error message, DB2 9.7 will automatically try to convert the data types to a common format—this is implicit casting. Implicit casting is also supported when using functions and procedures, and this makes it of particular interest to developers. For example, prior to DB2 9.7 the follow code would fail:

```
BEGIN
  DECLARE I INTEGER;
  SET I = '4';
  CALL DBMS_OUTPUT.PUT_LINE('I=' || VARCHAR(I));
END;
/

I=4
```

As mentioned, as of DB2 9.7, these restrictions are relaxed such that DB2 attempts to convert the data type to the most appropriate type. In the case of numeric values, this is usually straightforward. In some case, the conversion will result in truncation (such as an INTEGER to SMALLINT). For character string conversions to numbers, the process may not always work. If the string contains a number at the beginning, DB2 will attempt to convert it. If no numeric values are found, it will issue an error message, as shown here:

```
BEGIN
  DECLARE I INTEGER;
  SET I = 'A4';
  CALL DBMS_OUTPUT.PUT_LINE('I=' || VARCHAR(I));
END;
/

SQL0420N  Invalid character found in a character string
argument of the function "INTEGER".  SQLSTATE=22018
```

DB2 contains a large number of administrative functions that take multiple input parameters. For example, the EXPLAIN_GET_MSGS function can be used to get optimizer messages from the explain tables. Before DB2 9.7, each parameter had to be explicitly cast to the proper NULL value as follows:

```
SELECT MSG FROM
    TABLE(
        EXPLAIN_GET_MSGS( CAST (NULL AS VARCHAR(128)),
                          CAST (NULL AS TIMESTAMP),
                          CAST (NULL AS VARCHAR(128)),
                          CAST (NULL AS VARCHAR(128)),
                          CAST (NULL AS VARCHAR(64)),
                          CAST (NULL AS CHAR(1)),
                          CAST (NULL AS INTEGER),
                          CAST (NULL AS INTEGER),
                          CAST (NULL AS VARCHAR(33))
        )
    ) AS T ;
```

A developer would need to know the data type of each parameter type when coding the NULL values for the function. As mentioned, this task has been considerably simplified by having DB2 9.7 do the implicit casting as part of the function call. Here's an example:

```
SELECT MSG FROM
    TABLE(
        EXPLAIN_GET_MSGS( NULL,NULL,NULL,NULL,NULL,NULL,
        NULL,NULL,NULL)
    ) AS T ;
```

The automatic casting of data types also applies to untyped parameter markers and untyped NULL keywords almost anywhere in an SQL statement. This further simplifies the development of applications since developers don't need to add casting functions to their SQL.

Created Global Temporary Tables

Some types of workloads greatly benefit from the use of temporary tables. When a temporary table is created, any rows that are inserted or deleted from it are not logged, which results in much less overhead than required when using regular database tables. DB2 has long since supported temporary tables, but they are available only for the duration of the applications sessions—typically between the start of the transaction and its commit point.

For example, prior to DB2 9.7, the `DECLARE` statement was used to create temporary tables. The `DECLARE` statement is similar to the `CREATE` statement, except that `DECLARE` creates temporary tables that are used only during a session. Each temporary table is unique per user. This means that although an application may be shared among many users, the tables that are generated are *unique* for each user. To specify that this is a temporary table, the `SESSION` qualifier is assigned to the particular table that is being generated. The following SQL statement will create a temporary table that is valid for a single session only. The `DECLARE` statement specifies the name of the temporary table (T1) and how it's defined. In this example, the table is created based on the structure of another table (TRANSACTIONS). This simplifies the creation of these tables since you do not need to know the structure of the table from which you will be extracting data.

```
DECLARE GLOBAL TEMPORARY TABLE T1
    LIKE TRANSACTIONS
    ON COMMIT PRESERVE ROWS NOT LOGGED in SESSIONTEMP;
```

Selecting from this temporary table requires the use of the `SESSION` modifier in front of the table name, such as `SELECT * FROM SESSION.T1`.

NOTE: *A temporary table space needs to be created before you can use temporary tables.*

One difficulty with this approach of creating temporary tables is that it requires that the user know what the structure of the object should be. The preceding example used the `LIKE` clause to point to the structure of an existing table. However, not all users or applications will know how to create this object.

Instead of relying on the user to create the temporary object, DB2 9.7 now allows the use of global temporary tables. The syntax of the command changes slightly to `CREATE GLOBAL TEMPORARY TABLE` rather than `DECLARE GLOBAL TEMPORARY TABLE` as shown here:

```
CREATE GLOBAL TEMPORARY TABLE T1
    LIKE TRANSACTIONS
    ON COMMIT PRESERVE ROWS NOT LOGGED IN SESSIONTEMP;
```

A temporary table that was created with this syntax "lives" in the DB2 catalogs, while those created with the `DECLARE` statement couldn't be found in any catalogs. This allows the DBA to predefine the temporary objects along with any optimization features (indexes). Furthermore, the user or application no longer needs to `DECLARE` the temporary object in SQL; instead, the first time the object is referenced (for instance, in an `INSERT`), it will be created automatically for the session.

At the same time that this table is created and populated with data, any objects related to the object, such as indexes, will also be created. This removes the need for the user to know the structure of the table or to build any supporting indexes for it.

Now, to access this object, users no longer use the `SESSION` modifier; they can use their own schema to select from the table and could simply use a standard `SELECT` statement like this: `SELECT * FROM T1;`.

Named and Default Parameters

One of the most error-prone areas of writing SQL procedures is the passing of parameters. Errors occur when either the wrong number of parameters is supplied or they are passed in the wrong order. In DB2 9.7, a number of changes now affect how procedures can be defined and invoked. These changes include the ability to use default values for stored procedures and the ability to supply parameters in any order. These changes will make procedure writing much less error-prone.

In DB2 9.7, when defining a procedure, a developer can supply default values in the event they are not supplied by the user of the routine. For example, the following procedure uses a default value of 10% for a bonus if a value is not supplied:

```
CREATE TABLE PROD.EMPL
  (
  EMPNO   INTEGER,
  SALARY  INTEGER,
  BONUS   INTEGER
  );

CREATE PROCEDURE PROD.UPDATE_BONUS
  (
  EMPNO      INTEGER,
  SALARY     INTEGER DEFAULT 30000,
  BONUS_PCT  INTEGER DEFAULT 10
  )
```

```
BEGIN
  INSERT INTO PROD.EMPL VALUES(EMPNO, SALARY, SALARY *
  BONUS_PCT / 100);
END;
/
```

Assuming that the EMP table already exists, the following `CALL` statement will invoke the procedure with only two values, and it will use the 10% default value for the BONUS parameter:

```
CALL PROD.UPDATE_BONUS(1,20000);

CALL PROD.UPDATE_BONUS(2,20000,5);
SELECT * FROM PROD.EMPL;
```

```
EMPNO        SALARY        BONUS
----------   ----------    ----------
    1         20000          2000
    2         20000          1000
```

In addition to supplying default values for parameters, DB2 9.7 also allows a developer to change the order in which parameters are supplied to the procedure. A classic example of parameter mismatches occurs when a routine has a large number of parameters. Many of the parameters may have default values, or they could have `NULL` values. Most developers will code the call to the routine with multiple commas separating the `NULL` values—like so: `CALL PROCEDURE_NAME(,,,...,USEFUL_VALUE,...)`

However, being "out" by one position can dramatically change the results of the routine! So as of DB2 9.7, rather than a user having to guess the required position of a parameter, DB2 9.7 provides the new `PARAMETER=>VALUE` syntax that allows a user to name the parameter.

The `UPDATE_BONUS` procedure has three parameters: `EMPNO`, `SALARY`, and `BONUS`. Therefore, as of DB2 9.7, you could write a call to this routine like this:

```
CALL PROD.UPDATE_BONUS(EMPNO => 3, SALARY => 30000,
BONUS_PCT => 10);
```

Note that the order of the parameters in the `CALL` statement can now be changed so long as the proper parameter name is used. Here's an example:

```
CALL PROD.UPDATE_BONUS(BONUS_PCT => 10, EMPNO => 4,
SALARY => 40000);
```

This means a problematic procedure call with multiple `NULL` values could now be easily rewritten like this:

```
CALL PROCEDURE_NAME(USEFUL_VALUE => 1)
```

Autonomous Transactions

One of challenges when working with nested stored procedures is the effect of COMMIT and ROLLBACK commands. Prior to DB2 9.7, any stored procedure that was invoked by a trigger, function, or another stored procedure was under that object's transaction control. If the transaction decided to issue a ROLLBACK, all the work performed, including the changes made by the stored procedure, was also rolled back.

Normally when a transaction rolls back, its work (the changes made by all routines) should also be rolled back. In some cases, this may not be the desired result. For example, consider a scenario that involves the use of stored procedures for auditing UPDATE operations. Let's start with a trigger that has the following logic:

```
On update of salary
   Determine bonus by multiplying salary by 10%
   Update bonus field in employee record
   Call Audit_Update procedure to log the update
End Trigger
```

If the transaction that fires this trigger was cancelled, the audit record would also be removed from the system. To prevent the work done by the auditing stored procedure to be "protected" from this consequence, it must run in its own unit of work. You can do this in DB2 9.7 by defining the stored procedure with the new AUTONOMOUS keyword when using the CREATE PROCEDURE statement. Here's an example:

CREATE PROCEDURE AUDIT_BONUS() ... AUTONOMOUS

A procedure that you define with this new keyword runs within its own session, meaning that the procedure is independent of the calling procedure. If an autonomous procedure is successfully completed, the work is committed; if the procedure fails, the work is rolled back. In either case, the calling transaction is not affected.

SQL PL Support in Triggers, Functions, Blocks, and Procedures

Prior to DB2 9.7, restrictions were applied to what SQL PL could be used in stored procedures versus triggers, functions, and compound statement blocks. In DB2 9.7, SQL functions, triggers, and statement blocks can include or reference the following features:

- SQL PL statements, including `CASE` and `REPEAT` statements
- Support for declaring and referencing variables defined by local user-defined data types, including row data types, array data types, and cursor data types
- Cursor declarations
- Dynamic SQL
- Conditions
- Condition handlers

Updating the SQL PL syntax to be identical across all forms of procedural objects simplifies application development and reduces the potential for errors.

Record and Collection Types

Three different collection objects are available as part of DB2's PL/SQL support: *VARRAY*, *associative array*, and *record type*.

A `VARRAY` (also referred to as a *variable array*) is similar to the DB2 `ARRAY` type; however, a `VARRAY` is a set of ordered data elements with the same data type. Individual data items in the array can be referenced by using subscript notation within parentheses. Here's an example of the use of a `VARRAY`:

```
CREATE OR REPLACE PACKAGE TESTVARRAY
AS
   TYPE array_type IS VARRAY(5) OF NUMBER;
END;
/

DECLARE
    exp_array          testvarray.array_type;
    i                  INTEGER := 0;
BEGIN
    FOR i in 1..5 LOOP
        exp_array(i) := i;
    END LOOP;
END;
```

One important thing to note about type declarations is that the type must be defined within a PACKAGE body. The DECLARE statement then refers to the VARRAY definition found within the package.

An *associative array* is a collection type that associates a unique key with a value rather than indexing it with a number. The associative array is similar to the DB2 associative array, except that the type must be defined within a package. The TYPE IS TABLE OF statement is used to define an associative array type.

An associative array has the following characteristics:

- Must be defined before array variables of that array type can be declared.
- No defined limit on the number of elements in the array.
- Gaps can be included in the assignment of values to keys.
- An attempt to reference an array element that has not been assigned a value results in an exception.

The *record collection type* is a definition of a record that consists of one or more identifiers and their corresponding data types. You can create user-defined record types by using the TYPE IS RECORD statement. A record type definition is supported only in the CREATE PACKAGE or CREATE PACKAGE BODY statement.

A record variable is declared from a record type. The properties of the record, such as its field names and types, are inherited from the record type. Dot notation is used to reference fields in a record. The following example creates a record for a portion of the EMPLOYEE table:

```
CREATE OR REPLACE PACKAGE TEST_RECORD
   IS
      TYPE EMPLOYEE_TYPE IS RECORD (
         EMPNO EMPLOYEE.EMPNO%TYPE,
         LASTNAME EMPLOYEE.LASTNAME%TYPE
      );
END;
```

The use of the %TYPE anchor allows the definition of the EMPNO field to be tied directly to the EMPLOYEE.EMPNO column definition. This guarantees that the proper data type is used in the creation of the record.

If the application needs access to an EMPLOYEE_TYPE that contains all the elements of the EMPLOYEE table, it would be much simpler to use the %ROWTYPE attribute in the declaration section of a procedure, as shown here:

```
CREATE OR REPLACE PROCEDURE emp_sal_query (
    p_empno IN emp.empno%TYPE
)
IS
    r_emp emp%ROWTYPE;
BEGIN
  SELECT ename, job, hiredate, sal, deptno
    INTO r_emp.ename, r_emp.job, r_emp.hiredate,
    r_emp.sal, r_emp.deptno
    FROM emp WHERE empno = p_empno;
...
END
```

Cursor and Result Set Handling

You can use the built-in CURSOR data type or implement a user-defined cursor data type for use within applications, making it easier to work with result set data. A simple example of a CURSOR data type is shown in the following code segment:

```
DECLARE C1 cursor;
SET c1 = CURSOR FOR SELECT c1 FROM t1;
OPEN C1;
```

A CURSOR type can also be created in the system for use within procedures:

```
CREATE TYPE myRowType AS ROW(c1 INT, c2 INT, c3 INT);
CREATE TYPE myCursorType AS myRowType CURSOR;
```

A cursor variable can be used to access records from a table by using the FETCH cursor INTO variable syntax. In addition to manipulating the data, the cursor can also be checked against three conditions:

- **IS OPEN** Determines whether the cursor is in an open state.
- **IS NOT OPEN** Determines whether the cursor is closed.
- **IS FOUND** Determines whether the cursor contains rows after the execution of a FETCH statement. If the last FETCH statement executed was successful, the IS FOUND predicate value is TRUE. If the last FETCH statement executed resulted in a condition where rows were not found, the result is FALSE.

Additional cursor support was added in DB2 9.7 to allow cursors to be passed between routines and to work with cursor data when the SQL statement that defines the cursor is not known or might change.

Data Type Anchoring

Developers love the *anchored data type* declaration shortcut. Anchored declarations make it easy for developers to create applications without having to worry about the data types associated with the table. For instance, rather than having to figure out what the SALARY column's data type is, a developer could just anchor the variable directly to the table.

Here's a simple example that illustrates the usefulness of data type anchoring. We start by describing the existing EMPLOYEE table in the database:

```
DESCRIBE SELECT * FROM EMPLOYEE;

SQLTYPE_ID SQLTYPE           SQLLENGTH   SQLSCALE SQLNAME_DATA
---------- ------------      ----------  -------- ---------------
       452 CHARACTER                  6         0 EMPNO
       448 VARCHAR                   12         0 FIRSTNME
       453 CHARACTER                  1         0 MIDINIT
       448 VARCHAR                   15         0 LASTNAME
       453 CHARACTER                  3         0 WORKDEPT
       453 CHARACTER                  4         0 PHONENO
       393 TIMESTAMP                 19         0 HIREDATE
       453 CHARACTER                  8         0 JOB
       500 SMALLINT                   2         0 EDLEVEL
       453 CHARACTER                  1         0 SEX
```

If an application needed to manipulate the LASTNAME field, we would need to define this field as a VARCHAR(15). One problem associated with hard-coding the definition in an application is that the schema could evolve changing the definition of the data type, which would cause the application to fail due to the mismatch between the table and the local variable. Rather than leaving it up to chance, as of DB2 9.7, we can now anchor the variable to the column in the table as follows:

```
DECLARE
  EMPL_LASTNAME EMPLOYEE.LASTNAME%TYPE ;
BEGIN
  EMPL_LASTNAME :=
    (SELECT LASTNAME FROM EMPLOYEE WHERE EMPNO = '000010');
  DBMS_OUTPUT.PUT_LINE('LASTNAME=' || EMPL_LASTNAME);
END;

LASTNAME=HAAS
```

Exception Handling

Any error encountered in a program will stop execution unless an `EXCEPTION` section is present. The `EXCEPTION` section is used to trap and recover from errors. The following errors can be trapped:

- **CASE_NOT_FOUND** None of the cases in a `CASE` statement evaluates to `TRUE` and there is no `ELSE` condition.
- **CURSOR_ALREADY_OPEN** An attempt was made to open a cursor that is already open.
- **DUP_VAL_ON_INDEX** Duplicate values exist for the index key.
- **INVALID_CURSOR** An attempt was made to access an unopened cursor.
- **INVALID_NUMBER** The numeric value is invalid.
- **LOGIN_DENIED** The user name or password is invalid.
- **NO_DATA_FOUND** No rows satisfied the selection criteria.
- **NOT_LOGGED_ON** A database connection does not exist.
- **OTHERS** Any exception that has not been caught by a prior condition in the exception section.
- **SUBSCRIPT_BEYOND_COUNT** An array index is out of range or does not exist.
- **SUBSCRIPT_OUTSIDE_LIMIT** The data type of an array index expression is not assignable to the array index type.
- **TOO_MANY_ROWS** More than one row satisfied the selection criteria, but only one row is allowed to be returned.
- **VALUE_ERROR** The value is invalid.
- **ZERO_DIVIDE** Division by zero was attempted.

An exception block follows the body of the logic,—here's an example:

```
DECLARE
   ... variable definition ...
BEGIN
   ... logic ...
EXCEPTION
```

```
    WHEN exception-condition
    THEN handler-statement
    ... additional exception code ...
END;
```

If no error occurs, the block simply executes all the statements and the `EXCEPTION` statements are skipped. If an error does occur while executing a statement, the statement is abandoned and control passes to the `EXCEPTION` list. The list is searched for the first condition matching the error that occurred. If a match is found, the corresponding handler-statement is executed and control passes to the statement after `END`. If no match is found, the program stops executing.

Two additional statements, `RAISE_APPLICATION_ERROR` and `RAISE`, can be used to manipulate errors within a block. The `RAISE_APPLICATION_ERROR` procedure makes a user-defined code and error message available to the program, which can then be used to identify the exception. Here's an example:

```
RAISE_APPLICATION_ERROR(-20040,'Invalid salary for ' || p_empno);
```

The `RAISE` statement raises a previously defined condition. The condition is defined as part of the `DECLARE` block using the `EXCEPTION` keyword. Here'a an example:

```
CREATE OR REPLACE PROCEDURE raise_demo (inval NUMBER) IS
    evenno EXCEPTION;
BEGIN
    IF MOD(inval, 2) = 0 THEN
       RAISE evenno;
    END IF;
EXCEPTION
    WHEN evenno THEN
       dbms_output.put_line(TO_CHAR(inval) || ' is even');
END raise_demo;
```

CONSTANT Support

A new feature introduced for PL SQL language support is the ability to define constants within a procedure, a function, or an anonymous block. As part of the variable definition, a new `CONSTANT` keyword specifies that the variable value is constant. A default expression must be assigned, and a new value cannot be assigned to the variable within the application program. Here's an example:

```
DECLARE PI CONSTANT NUMBER := 3.14159;
```

Attempting to modify a constant from within a procedure will result in an error code, as shown here:

```
DECLARE
   PI CONSTANT NUMBER := 3.14159;
BEGIN
   PI := 3.14;
END;

SQL0206N  "PI" is not valid in the context where it is
used.  LINE NUMBER=1.  SQLSTATE=42703
```

The CONSTANT keyword is another example of the large number of new SQL features that were introduced in DB2 9.7 to help improve the productivity of the application developer. This chapter touches many of these features, but there are many more to be found in the remaining chapters of the book.

7
The Even More Available DB2

In this chapter, we talk about some of the things that make the DB2 server (referred to as DB2 in this chapter) even more available in the DB2 9.7 release. Availability means more than just a server being up; for example, if your service level agreement (SLA) dictates that expected query response times are seconds and the server is returning queries in minutes; that's an availability issue. (Of course, within that context, we could have packed a lot of features into this chapter—but we digress.) Here, we'll detail the upcoming read-on-standby technology (which should be available in DB2 9.7 Fix Pack 1 or shortly thereafter), performance improvements such as scan sharing, the statement concentrator, and core resiliency improvements. All these technologies are designed to get you more out of your DB2 database.

High Availability Disaster Recovery Enhancements

High Availability Disaster Recovery (HADR) was introduced in DB2 8.2, and since then has become the standard for turnkey availability solutions. In fact, we could make you an HADR expert and get you to serious high availability (HA) in less than a day. It's outside the scope of this book to detail HADR and its benefits, but we do want to tell you about some upcoming enhancements that we think you are going to like.

The DB2 High Availability Value Proposition

The DB2 product has been on a continuum of delivering high value and effective availability capabilities for a number of versions. For example, DB2 9 removed the requirement to license any Feature Packs on a standby machine—you just had to partially license the standby server per the DB2 high availability licensing rules. What's more, DB2 9 gave you a free two server license for Tivoli System Automation for Multiplatforms (SA-MP) so you could automate HADR failover or just set up an old-fashion HA server cluster of your own.

DB2 9.5 not only made HADR free in DB2 Workgroup, but it took the SA-MP code and drove it into the core of DB2 such that DB2 has an integrated cluster facility that's available for pretty much all DB2 editions. If you compare this to other products in the marketplace, you'll find it a unique value proposition unparalleled in flexibility and use. What's more, DB2 9.5 changed the high availability taxonomy from a simple `active/idle` label to `hot/warm/cold`. Without getting into the details (which are available on the Web), the new `cold` designation allows you to configure *some* high availability environments without any associated license charges on the standby server. For example, if you use the integrated SA-MP clustering software that's built into DB2 to create a `hot/cold` cluster, you don't have to pay for the standby server or the clustering software. So while some vendors' HA offerings perpetrate value with a set number of days of free failover, DB2 would be free forever. Talk to your IBM representative for more information.

In DB2 9.7, if you buy DB2 Express with an FTL or a SERVER license, you get use of the HADR and SA-MP features for free on top of all the other benefits mentioned here. (If you license DB2 Express using an Authorized User or PVU license, you can get HADR and Tivoli SA-MP only by purchasing the associated High Availability Feature Pack.)

If you trace the HA value proposition over the last half decade in DB2, you'll find a continuum of enhanced value, and when you consider the world's current economic state, you can see how it enriches the value of your DB2 solution.

Enhanced Support for Large Objects with HADR

DB2 9.7 offers enhanced support for large objects (LOBs) with respect to how LOBs are logged, compared to DB2 9.5. For example, with DB2 9.5, if you used

LOBs with HADR, they were limited to 1GB because the LOB had to be logged to participate in an HADR configuration. DB2 9.5 Fix Pack 4 introduced a new configuration parameter called BLOCKNONLOGGED, which prevented any non-logged operation from occurring: this was particularly useful in an HADR or log-shipping environment.

Of course, DB2 supports LOBs of up to 2GB, and this creates a potential impediment mismatch between your HA requirements and your applications. In an up-and-coming DB2 9.7 Fix Pack, this limitation will be lifted, and applications that need to work with any sized LOBs can be configured to participate in an HADR environment.

Read on Standby Support for HADR

A noteworthy enhancement expected for HADR is the ability for a standby HADR server to support read operations: this is called *read-on-standby (RoS)*. In previous versions of DB2, this was not possible in an HADR cluster. With HADR enabled for the RoS feature, an HADR standby database is functional not only for high availability or disaster recovery purposes, but also for running read-only workloads.

The RoS solution allows customers to:

- Distribute read workloads across both servers in the HADR cluster: applications explicitly connect to the appropriate server to run those applications
- Run read-only workloads with minimal impact to the standby system's primary role of HA or disaster recovery
- Increase capacity of the HADR solution and help spread reporting costs across the entire cluster with a simple switch

An example of an HADR RoS standby environment is shown in Figure 7-1.

In Figure 7-1, you can see that the primary server (Server 1) looks the same as the primary server in earlier releases of the HADR technology. When this feature is delivered, assuming you've enabled the RoS capability, the user initiating Session 3 on Server 2 can perform read-only work on that server's database, and that's very different than what could be done in earlier versions.

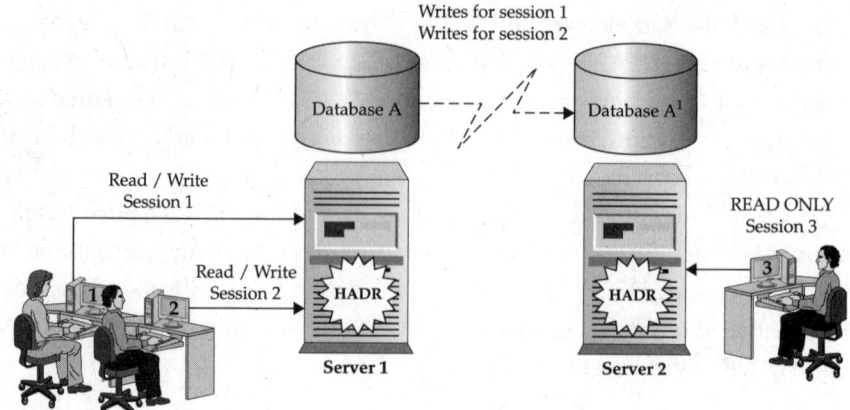

Figure 7.1 *An HADR cluster reading data on the HADR standby server.*

To keep the database synchronized, even when the RoS feature is enabled, the standby database is perpetually rolling forward logged operations received from the primary. This state was referred to as ROLLFORWARD before this feature was introduced. When HADR RoS becomes available, the new name for this status will be *Standby*; once readers are enabled on the standby, the database status will change to *Active Standby*. You can find the status for all your HADR configured databases using the GET SNAPSHOT FOR ALL command, as well as using some of the views and table functions available for this purpose in DB2.

To enable RoS for an HADR cluster you will set the secondary server's DB2_HADR_ROS registry variable to ON (this registry variable will require you to recycle the instance for the changes to take effect). The ability to read data on the secondary server is supported during all HADR synchronization modes (SYNC, NEARSYNC, and ASYNC) and most HADR states (LOCAL CATCHUP is the only state not supported). All RoS queries must request the Uncommitted Read (UR) isolation level to read data on the standby server; in fact, if a statement requests a higher isolation level, the application will receive an SQL error. You'll be able to override this default behavior using the DB2_STANDBY_ISO registry variable so that if a statement requests a stricter isolation level (for example, Cursor Stability), the request will be downgraded to UR *without* any warning or notification. If you set this variable on the secondary server and it becomes the primary server, this registry setting will be ignored and all isolation levels will be honored. This registry setting also supersedes any isolation method you may request—for example, using the `SET CURRENT ISOLATION` statement.

Since the main goal of HADR is to provide HA or disaster recovery, if you issue a `TAKEOVER` command on an active standby server, all connections will be terminated (no matter how close they are to being completed) and new connections will be blocked (any application attempting to connect during this time will receive an `SQL1776N` error).

We want to remind you that your main purpose is HA or disaster recovery when it comes to an HADR implementation. Keep that in mind and test your recovery time objective (RTO) to ensure that it falls within your SLA. For example, an On-Line Transaction Processing (OLTP) application is characterized by normalization and minimal indexes for the fastest possible transactional throughput. Now consider some analyst running reports on the secondary server—a server that doesn't have as many purpose-built schema objects (such as indexes) to speed up reporting applications because keeping the primary server as nimble and quick as possible is the main goal. The query workload on the standby is likely to result in a lot of table scans and a lot of inefficient activity within the buffer pool. In addition, having a number of live connections on the standby database could cause delays in the takeover process as these connections need to be terminated in flight. We're not saying that you shouldn't open up the standby for query—we're just saying that you should test your recovery process so that you don't encounter any surprises in the wee hours of some Saturday morning.

You need to be aware of a few things (beyond the fact that you are using the secondary server actively, which has licensing implications) if you plan to use an HADR standby server for query workloads when it initially becomes available. For example, you won't be able to connect to the database while the standby server is replaying data definition language (DDL) statements or performing maintenance operations. Specifically, when an HADR standby starts the replay of a DDL or maintenance operation, it enters into something called the *replay-only window*. To enter this operational window, the HADR standby needs to terminate all connections and block any new ones. When the standby leaves this window, new connections and queries are once again allowed. For example, if you had a query running on the active standby server, and a statistics collection was run on the primary server, when that logged operation flowed to the standby, your application would terminate and you would have to reconnect to the database when the maintenance operation completed and start your work again.

> **NOTE:** For a complete list of activities that will force off current readers on the standby server, refer to the DB2 Information Center.

The RoS capability will help you wring more and more value out of your DB2 servers when it becomes available. One obvious example is that reporting can be off-loaded from the primary database to the secondary, and the utilization rates of the standby server can be driven to higher and higher value. But other benefits can also be realized. For example, perhaps you periodically need to perform validation that data is synchronized within the configuration; with RoS, you can perform this validation without having to convert the standby to primary with a graceful takeover.

Scan Sharing

A typical data warehouse environment often involves queries that produce a lot of I/O. Since disk access is much slower than memory access, the key to an efficient and high-performing data warehouse is to reduce I/Os as much as possible (that's why applications tend to run faster when DB2 compression is used—reduced I/O). It's well known that for OLTP systems, you want to have as much data resident in the buffer pool as possible; however, in a data warehouse, your tables are likely too large to fit completely in memory. For this reason, when multiple users are running large scans simultaneously, it's unlikely that you'll able to maintain a high buffer pool hit ratio. This is precisely why features such as the database partitioning feature, compression, range partitioning, multidimensional clustering (MDC) tables, and other I/O reducing techniques are essential in data warehouse environments.

Even in consideration of the aforementioned performance-boosting technologies, many users are likely to be accessing the same tables (or subsets of the same tables) and performing large sequential scans over the same data pages; *however* the buffer pool hit ratios will still remain low. For example, consider a scenario in which two users (USER1 and USER2) are both performing a full table scan on table T1. Assume that T1 contains 1 million pages. USER1 will read the table starting at page number 1 and continue reading until it reads page number 1,000,000. Now assume that USER2 submits a query that performs a scan of the same table, but it hits the database halfway through USER1's table scan. At this point, USER2 is now starting to read page 1 while USER1 is now reading page 500,000. Given that the buffer pool for this table may not be large enough to hold all of its pages, it's likely the case that USER2 will now be performing I/O operations for pages that USER1 *has already read* from disk. The result? In some cases, both users could end up reading 1 million pages each, for a total of 2 million page reads. Quite simply, prior to DB2 9.7, USER2's triggered scan wasn't smart enough to realize that eventually it was going to need the pages that USER1's scan was currently reading.

DB2 9.7 boosts the performance of these types of operations by introducing a new technology known as *scan sharing*. Scan sharing can dramatically reduce I/O operations in a data warehouse environment and therefore improve throughput and increase performance. Now consider the example in the preceding paragraph with DB2 9.7. In this case, DB2's scan sharing algorithm notices that both users are scanning the same set of pages and will intelligently piggy-back USER2 onto USER1's current scan position by creating a *scan sharing group* (which other scanners are free to join as well). Specifically, when this example runs in a DB2 9.7 environment, USER2 will actually start reading table T1 at page 500,000. USER2 will then read through to page 1,000,000 together with USER1, thereby sharing the I/O operations and leveraging the work USER1 has to do to fetch required data pages into the buffer pool. When both users have read page 1,000,000, USER1 is done and USER2's scanner will go back and read the pages it missed—namely, it will start at page 1 and read only to page 500,000. By working together, these two users have reduced the number of I/O operations and improved the buffer pool hit ratio.

This example shows two users to keep it simple; there's no limit on the number of users that can scan share. In fact, the more users scanning the same data, the greater the potential benefit. DB2 will automatically assign scanners to groups in an effort to keep similar scanners (who are scanning at similar speeds) together so that they can all progress more quickly—so DB2 can support multiple scan groups. In addition, some really cool intelligence is available in the scan sharing algorithm such that if a scanner in a scan group is going too slow and holding back the other scanners in the group, DB2 will automatically remove that scanner from the group so that the others in the group can work together more quickly. Similarly, if one scanner is going much faster than the group is capable of, DB2 will automatically remove that scanner from the group so that it can speed ahead of the others and finish its work.

Scan sharing works for table scans, range partition scans, and MDC lock and block index scans. The best part is that scan sharing is all automatic (a theme to the DB2 9.7 release). You don't need to set configuration parameters to turn scan sharing on or off, and you don't have to define what scanners go into which scanner groups. DB2 9.7 manages all of this on your behalf to deliver the best results possible in multi-user data warehouse environments. To monitor scan sharing that may be occurring in your database, you can use the new `-scansharing` option in the `db2pd` tool.

Statement Concentrator

The DB2 9.7 statement concentrator improves statement compilation time by using statements in the dynamic statement cache and stripping out their literal values. The statement concentrator is useful in environments characterized by a high volume of dynamic SQL statements that are identical except for the value of literals in the statements. Without the statement concentrator, each different literal value requires that a new access plan be compiled, and this can consume a significant amount of system resources. For example, assume that DB2 compiles and executes an SQL statement such as this:

`SELECT * FROM EMPLOYEE WHERE WORKDEPT='A00' AND SALARY > 50000;`

When a similar request hits the database server (for example, `SELECT * FROM EMPLOYEE WHERE WORKDEPT='D01' AND SALARY > 30000;`), DB2 attempts to find this statement in the package cache.

From a DB2 perspective, both statements are different since they compile into different access plans because of the `SALARY` predicates. When DB2 attempts to look for "similar" statements in the package cache, it won't find a match, and therefore DB2 needs to compile each statement separately and then run them. As long as subsequent statements come in with different values for `WORKDEPT` and `SALARY`, DB2 can't reuse any of the previous optimizations that it's done. The solution to this problem is the new DB2 9.7 *statement concentrator*.

You turn on the statement concentrator in DB2 9.7 with the database-level configuration parameter `STMT_CONC` using a command similar to the following: `UPDATE DB CFG FOR sample USING stmt_conc literals immediate;` (updating this parameter requires that you recycle the database). Once the statement concentrator has been enabled, any subsequent statements that come into the DB2 compiler will be checked for constants. If any constants are found, they will be stripped out and replaced with parameter markers (?). For example, the first SQL statement mentioned earlier in this section would now look like this:

SELECT * FROM EMPLOYEE WHERE WORKDEPT=? AND SALARY>?;

When DB2 executes the first SQL statement, it would supply the values 'A00' and 50000 to get the proper result, since that's what the application passed as literals to the database. The second SQL statement would be rewritten using parameter markers as well (resulting in a cache hit, since the two SQL statements are now identical), and the values 'D01' and 30000 would be substituted for the parameter markers when the second SQL statement is executed.

The performance gains from using a statement concentrator can be significant, especially if the workloads use constants and issue the same type of SQL repeatedly.

For business intelligence and warehousing workloads, the use of the statement concentrator may not be as useful. These environments are characterized by statements that tend to be complex and not repeated as often. In addition, the constants could be of use to the optimizer when determining the access plans, so removing them before compilation could hinder optimization.

Finally, it's worthy noting that the Optim pureQuery technology has a client-side version of literal replacement. Depending on the scenario, one can be more advantageous than the other; however, that's outside the scope of this book.

Resilience Improvements

Remaining operational, especially during peak business hours, is a primary objective of every business. Many components are involved in achieving this. This section focuses on dealing with the infrequent, but critical, error conditions that can lead to a DB2 outage. DB2 9.7 includes enhancements that increase its ability to deal with certain critical errors, traps, and crashes, leading to higher resiliency. At the end of the day, after dealing gracefully with a critical error or trap condition, a DB2 9.7 database instance might still need to be recycled—but this can now be scheduled after peak business hours at a time of your choosing. DB2 9.7's resilience improvements focus on three main areas: resiliency for DB2 read errors, resiliency for traps, and diagnostic log rotation.

Resiliency for Read Errors

Prior to DB2 9.7, when a DB2 agent encountered an error when reading a page, a critical terminating error resulted and the database instance was shutdown. To make DB2 more resilient, DB2 9.7 can tolerate many of these read errors and handle them more gracefully than in previous versions. Instead of the DB2 instance shutting down, it will return new SQL codes to the application and log appropriate administration errors. The DB2 instance remains available. For example, instead of a read error resulting in the immediate shutdown of the database, DB2 9.7 can gracefully deal with this kind of error and return an error code to the application (such as an `SQL1655E` read error or an `SQL1656E` page inconsistency error), allowing DB2 to maintain its consistency and continue to operate.

Resiliency for Trapped Threads

Before DB2 9.7, when a severe memory trap occurred for a DB2 agent, the usual result is that the instance would shutdown. DB2 9.7 introduces the ability to handle these kinds of thread traps and automatically perform rollback and cleanup operations for a troubled agent—all while allowing the DB2 instance to remain online. As of DB2 9.7, if a trap is encountered, DB2 determines whether it's safe to sustain the trap after collecting all the relevant diagnostic information. If DB2 can sustain the trap, the faulty agent will rollback its transaction and suspend itself. Resiliency for trapped threads is controlled in a way similar to resiliency for DB2 read errors; it's on by default in DB2 9.7.

Diagnostic and Administration Notify Log Rotation

An infrequent, yet severe, outage inducing an error can occur when diagnostic logs are allowed to grow indefinitely, eventually overflowing the file system. At that point, DB2 cannot continue because it cannot guarantee the consistency of the database since it doesn't have any log space. To remove this possibility, DB2 9.7 offers the ability to rotate diagnostic and administration notify logs.

Using the new instance-level `DIAGSIZE` configuration parameter, DBAs define a business policy that dictates the maximum disk space (in MBs) that the diagnostic and administration notification logs can consume (the limit that both log files can consume when added together). The default value is 0, which means that these log files can grow as large as they want (the behavior prior to DB2 9.7).

For example, if you want to ensure that the combined space consumed by the diagnostic and administration logs never take up more than 512MB of disk space, you can issue the command: `DB2 UPDATE DBM CFG DIAGSIZE 512` (changing this parameter requires that you recycle the DB2 instance). At this point forward, all diagnostic and administration notification messages would be recorded into multiple rotating log files; specifically into the file with the largest index number. In DB2 9.7, these log files are numbered using the format: `db2diag.#.log` (for the diagnostic logs) and `instance.#.nfy` (for the administration logs). The DB2 9.7 naming convention for these logs uses # to identify the log number. The naming starts at 0 and is incremented every time a new log is created to a maximum of 9 (giving you a maximum of ten log files). When DB2 fills the tenth log file, the oldest log file is pruned (think circular logging for recovery—it's kind of the same thing) and new log files are created. The number of `db2dialog.#.log` files and `instance.#.nfy` files created before a rotation will never exceed ten.